shock[1] (shŏk) *n.* **1.** Something, as an event or encounter, that jars the mind or emotions as if with a violent, unexpected blow.

MARRIAGE SHOCK

"Barbara, a jeweler in Mary Gaitskill's 1988 short story 'Connection,' tries to explain to her old friend Susan why her twelve-year marriage has ended. She says it isn't that she and John didn't know each other very well, nor that she doesn't love John anymore. 'I'm not sure how to describe it,' she says. 'It was like everything that supported the relationship was coming from the outside.' Even worse, she says, 'it seemed as if our most intimate conversations were based on what we were supposed to be saying, and what we were supposed to be. Nothing seemed to come directly from us.'

"The first moment a new wife feels this odd remove—her words not coming from her own soul, her real life suddenly clashing with the expectation of what that life is supposed to be—that is a moment I call marriage shock. . . ."

MARRIAGE
SHOCK

MARRIAGE
SHOCK

The Transformation
of Women into Wives

DALMA HEYN

Delta
Trade Paperbacks

A Delta Book
Published by
Dell Publishing
a division of
Bantam Doubleday Dell Publishing Group, Inc.
1540 Broadway
New York, New York 10036

Portions of Chapter 9 were originally published as "The Affair, '96: Why Women Are Always to Blame" in *Mirabella* (March/April 1996) and portions of Chapter 10 were originally published as "Why Girls Don't Wanna Have Fun" in *New Woman* (June 1995).

ISBN: 0-385-32402-2

Reprinted by arrangement with Villard Books

Manufactured in the United States of America
Published simultaneously in Canada

April 1998

10 9 8 7 6 5 4 3 2 1

BVG

To my husband, Richard

CONTENTS

INTRODUCTION

MY FATHER IS my mother's third husband. Her first two husbands were Hollywood celebrities. After her second husband had died and she decided to marry my father, a substantial but not famous magazine editor from New York, there was a prevailing sense among their friends that this marriage would last about as long as a feature film. At a party celebrating their engagement, a reporter said as much to her.

"How did a guy like Ernie Heyn win a glorious creature like yourself?" he asked.

"He swept me off my knees," she replied.

IN ONE REMARK, the history of the Western world. At its center was women's profound desire to be married—whether for the first time or the third, in 1947 or in 1997. Despite recent trends suggesting a shift in behavior—marriage at a later age, motherhood without marriage—over 90 percent of all American women will wed at least once before the age of forty-nine. And while 65 percent of these marriages will end in divorce, the number of weddings will simply increase, since three quarters of all these parted partners—five out of six men and three out of four women—will remarry within four years. Widows will marry again, too, on average within seven years of their spouse's death.

There are, in other words, more women getting married more often than ever before.

We love marriage. We love to dream about it, prepare for it, enter it, exit it, and do it all over again. What do women talk about within ten minutes of meeting each other? Marriage. Upcoming marriages. Outgoing marriages. The marriages of movie stars. Marriages from hell. Our last marriage. The marriage we will have if we ever marry again. The glory of marriage. The agony of it.

One of our favorite discussions revolves around the notion of marriage as a female-designed trap into which reluctant bachelors fall, as if this venerable institution were women's natural habitat. Yet it could not be *less* natural for many women today. The average young woman—working, assertive personally and professionally—is comfortable with independence, employment, autonomy, and multiple sexual relationships. She began having sex, according to the newest Kinsey Institute Report, between the (median) ages of sixteen and seventeen. If she marries at the age of twenty-seven, then, she will have been making love—with one man or several, simultaneously or serially, alone or cohabiting—for a decade. She is as used to pleasure as to pleasing, and envisions having both in equal measure in an egalitarian marital relationship.

Yet we send this sexually experienced modern woman to the altar the way we sent her virginal, voteless, and homebound great grandmother: with revelry and relief, and the vague, romantic prayer that if she has chosen Mr. Right right, she will, sure enough, live happily ever after. The odds are against it. But as a culture we continue to support, with our hopes, our silence, and our denial of crucial new realities, a relentlessly dewy-eyed picture of marriage.

This book questions that picture, along with the assumptions and myths that support it. Becoming a wife is, after all, one of three critical life changes for a woman. It commands as profound an adjustment psychologically and emotionally as her earlier transition into puberty did and as motherhood will. Much is written about the dramatic transformations associated with both adolescence and motherhood, but there is little about the dramatic transition to wifehood. While my conclusions are ultimately optimistic, I found that even to inquire about marriage, to ask whether as presently conceived it is a healthful environment for women, truly hospitable to us, almost always elicits apprehension: "Does this mean you're against marriage? That you're going to tell people not to get married?" No, I'm for marriage. I'm married myself, happily. But marriage is more than just the lifelong, committed companionship of a man and a woman. It is an institution. And I cannot think of a single institution—the church, the military, the academy—that has ever truly welcomed women's voices, nor one that even truly welcomes women at all. *Marriage* doesn't truly welcome women. If we ignore this, as if marital relationships were independent from the seas in which they set sail, we will remain mystified when they continue to veer off course as frequently as they do, and end up sinking.

I wrote my last book, *The Erotic Silence of the American Wife*, because of findings that also violated some of our most treasured ideals. Wives were having affairs earlier in their marriages, and more often than ever before. How could this be? Married *men* may have affairs, but married *women?* Don't women thrive in marriage? Aren't we more moral, more monogamous, than men? Could it be, moreover, that something good might come out of doing something the culture deems very bad—in fact, the very worst thing a woman can do?

I listened to women speak about the unspeakable, straying from the sanctified framework inside which they're supposed to flourish. Far more disturbing than listening to women speak about their affairs, I found, was hearing them talk about marriage. For although adultery is the "worst" act a woman can commit and getting married is the "best," I'm not sure which extreme, transgression or idealization, is harder for women to tell the truth about, or more daunting to penetrate. They're two sides of the same rusty old coin: heads, there's a bad woman, and tails, a good one. What bad women say, we don't want to listen to, and good women can't speak openly without fear of being called bad.

So if I wanted to look deeply into women's experience of marriage, I had to make it clear to the women I spoke with that I was calling off the dogs of "good" and "bad" and declaring a verbal, moral armistice; that we were in a magic, safe sanctuary where the usual judgments were unwelcome. Without that assurance, all I'd hear is silence.

We know what wives' badness leads to: Think of all the literature, all those novels and operas and movies, brimming with all that passion and outrage and death! Think of how many cultures still stone an adulteress! But a woman's *goodness*—well, what I've discovered is that it is even more deadly for a wife: It kills her as surely as any sword or onrushing train, only more slowly, silently.

MY OWN GIRLHOOD struggle with "goodness" fuels my passion for this complicated, subversive topic. I know that when I hear society's condemning language of right and wrong—defining what kind of woman behaves this way or that way in marriage, or what kind of woman questions marriage, or avoids it, or has trouble being herself in it, or suffers and endures it, or tries to change it, or leaves it altogether—I viscerally recognize just what women are running from. This very language itself, the very "morality" greeting them in marriage, kills the pleasure and fun women naturally find in their love relationships, the pleasure and fun marriage promises. This is deeply paradoxical and, on the face of it, makes no sense: When women enter marriage, ostensibly the place where they may most freely express and enjoy their sexuality, many instead find it captured, held, and immobilized. They soon feel that they have lost touch with something in themselves, or are hiding it, or are forbidden from revealing it. The culture's cherished belief that marriage is where women flourish, then, is simply at odds with the reality of women's distress, disorientation, and, yes, depression in it—and their departure from it. As we will see in these pages.

I'M INTERESTED IN goodness, all right, but not what's good *in* or good *about* wives. I want to know what's good *for* a wife in her marriage. What would it take for marriage to welcome her voice, her needs, and her desires? What creates a new kind of marriage in which a wife's creativity, her spontaneity, her spirit—in the broadest sense, her sexuality—are all set free?

These are not questions we have historically been concerned with. We'd all rather debate what a "good" wife is, whether she's doing good things for others—particularly her husband and children, as we expect her to. But while many women are saying they want marriage as much as ever, and need what it offers in order to feel loved, respected, and valued, they're finding that they're giving up too much, and that what they're getting isn't all they want.

What are they giving up? At what point? And why, now, still, can't we understand what it is, or value it, and then help them keep it? What are we asking a new wife to hide, or not say, or not know; that is, what do her and my questions about love and marriage threaten? I hope this book smashes some of the structural walls of this very old and revered institution and lets in the light that has transformed every other part of women's lives.

MARRIAGE
SHOCK

1

Matrimorphosis: Women into Wives

> She felt that she had entered a new world, some unknown
> planet entirely different from anything she had known
> and loved; everything in her life and thoughts was upset.
> This strange question occurred to her; Did she love her
> husband? He suddenly appeared a stranger who she
> hardly knew. Three months earlier she had not been
> aware of his existence; now she was his wife. What did it
> all mean? Why should one fall into marriage so quickly, as
> into an abyss suddenly yawning before one's feet?
>
> —GUY DE MAUPASSANT
> *A Woman's Life*

"SO HOW *ARE* you?" Ella asks her married sister, three months
after the family wedding that dazzled two hundred guests. Two
months earlier, still recovering from the elaborate celebration,
still unwrapping toasters and roasting pans, Judy had answered
the same question: "Terrific." Now she tries to assure her baby
sister with feigned good cheer. "How am I?" she repeats, throwing her head back the way she used to when she still smoked, in-

haling air between tight lips, taking the question into her lungs. Then she looks up again, back from thought and into her sister's eyes: "I'm okay. Really. Fine." She smiles. Ella catches the deflation in her sister's voice, notices the falseness of just one quick gesture—the way Judy intended to look straight at her when she exhaled but dodged her eyes for just a split second. But she doesn't want to pry.

Ella is not used to having to be careful around her sister. They had always been so open: From the time they were young teenagers, they would shut their bedroom door and talk to each other. No topic was taboo. When one was in love, she told the other one all the details. When one was angry at the other, she never kept it pent up; they'd always battle it out. Sometimes they hated each other, but always, always, they talked.

"HOW'S JACK?" ELLA asks a few weeks later, trying again.

"He's great," Judy says, as if talking to their mother. "Working too hard, of course, but loving it. Or at least loving being a good earner and provider."

Hating the sharpening chill that nips their conversation, Ella takes a breath. "You know, sweetie . . . we never discuss Jack in any real way."

"What do you mean?"

"We only talk about how hard he works, what a good father he'll be, what kind of job he's up for. We never talk about anything that has to do with *you*. I mean, what's it like being married to this man? What's *he* like, inside? You're my sister, and suddenly you and I are locked in this conversation that could be taking place between two acquaintances: 'Oh really? You paid the mortgage? Well, swell! I'm off to the cleaners. Have a great day!' " And then she blurts it out: "I feel as if you're afraid to talk to me about what you really feel."

"Oh," Judy says sadly.

Ella knows her sister so well. She knows that tone of voice—the muted, childlike tone that betrays Judy's feelings the instant she utters the first word. And today what Ella hears is confusion and sadness. "Speak to me!" she wants to shout. "What's happened to you? Do you want me to come get you? Take you away from this thing, whatever it is, that's come over you?"

Judy doesn't know what has come over her. Sometimes she thinks nothing has, it's just that she's married now and her allegiance has shifted; she doesn't want to say anything that would betray her husband. Or maybe it's just that people who aren't married—Ella included—can't understand that things really are different, that marriage is not just a piece of paper. It has changed her life.

If she sounds different, well . . . maybe that's how a wife sounds.

Other times, though, Judy longs for Ella to rescue her, to break through the film of ice that is slowly encasing her. Why should things be *so* different that she can't speak about them? She wants to cry out to Ella, "Yes, do get through; I *am* feeling strange, tell me why, push me to try. How can I have everything I've ever wanted and still feel this way? Make me speak; don't leave me! Something *is* wrong."

What gets her most of all is this feeling that whatever it is she does feel cannot be shared any longer. Even her closest friends and family, even her beloved sister, can't understand. It's her discomfiture alone, and so unexpected she can't even find the language to describe the strain. Not only can't she admit it, she doesn't even know what "it" is. She keeps thinking, I'm a new bride, for God's sake. When will I ever be happier? Yet the core of that happiness eludes her. She feels deeply, profoundly, *not like herself.*

THIS IS WHAT Tracy wore to the annual Christmas party given by Tom's firm: a little cropped red mohair cardigan over the tight, short black leather skirt she credits with helping to "conquer" Tom, suede shoes with a tiny Louis heel—elegant but sturdy enough for dancing—and a miniature satin backpack, so her hands could be free. She wore her cropped, auburn hair very spiky, punked out the way she liked it, with just a touch of lavender in the fine wisps at her hairline.

She was twenty-five. She had looked forward to this party every year since she'd begun dating Tom four years before, because there was always a terrific band, and while her fiancé didn't dance, two of his closest colleagues, Jake and Peter, were as fanatic rock and rollers as she was.

When Tracy and Tom arrived, each went to a different part of the bar. She poured herself some eggnog; Tom got a double scotch on the rocks. Tracy checked to make sure her dance partners were in sight and waited impatiently for the band to start up. "Well, it was nice knowing you," Tom said amiably when it did.

"So?" Tom said when they got back to his apartment. "Did you have fun?"

"I don't know who Fred is, but he sure can dance."

"Fred is the mailboy," her fiancé said. He pulled her to him and stroked the soft leather of her skirt. "I love your hair like this," he said. "And I love this skirt."

"I know that," she said. "It's a magic garment that lets me dance with lots of men all night and still go home with the man I adore. I owe it all to this skirt."

What Tracy wore to that same Christmas party a year later, the year she married Tom, was harder to choose. Over Tom's protests, she had given away her treasured little black leather skirt, so that was out. She rejected a little sweater dress as too short, too sexy. She decided to wear a proper, more businessy suit—a plummy tweed one with flecks of gray in it.

When Jake came over to ask her to dance, she went, but she was worried about Tom, who, she noticed, was drinking much more than he normally did. "See you later, honey," she said as she left, managing to take his scotch with her, as if absentmindedly, to the dance floor.

"Why didn't you dance more?" Tom asked her when they got home.

"The band wasn't as good as usual," she said. That was true enough, but it wasn't the real reason. She didn't quite *know* the answer; all she knew was that she had fretted through most of the evening. The whole party had a different feel this year. She'd vowed to spend more time getting to know Tom's boss, and had ended up having a rather labored, self-conscious conversation with him—all the while wistfully aware of the music in the background. At "I Heard It Through the Grapevine" she wound her way over to Fred, but she was distracted. Tom, she thought again, was eating too much.

Should she really be dancing when she could be getting to know the people he worked with? Did she look inane lip-synching "On Broadway" in her knee-length business suit? She didn't know whether she felt too old, or too young, or what. She left the dance floor and went back to Tom's boss.

At this year's Christmas party, Tracy, now twenty-seven and married over a year, didn't dance at all. She was riveted by the secretaries, standing in separate groups. How sexy and lively they looked, so different from the wives! Tired secretary-and-boss jokes danced in her head. Jake and Peter waved. "Come on, Trace," they said as they passed her. "You're missing the best band yet!" She told them she was a little tired.

"Face it, you don't dance anymore!" Jake said. "You're getting old."

"Sure I dance!" Tracy protested. "Later, okay? After I get myself some food."

ANTONIA USED TO tell Jonathan all her sexual feelings. Her frankness about every detail of what she was experiencing was a quality Jonathan loved about her from the moment they began having sex—which was after the fourth date, a year before they married, each for the second time. Yet Antonia says this sexual openness was something she'd achieved only in her relationship with Jonathan, something she had with him right from the beginning, a gift, an amazing alliance that allowed her to be herself—hungry, experimental, *dirty*—for the first time in her life.

It was part of what made their relationship so fine, she felt, and for her it was hard-earned.

Never before had she felt so free to speak, so *able* to speak, during sex. When other men had asked, "What do you like?" she had mumbled words that mirrored whatever they were doing—less a nice-girl tactic to please her partner, she thought, than shyness and a deep uncertainty about what she *did* like.

But with Jonathan, she had found herself, from the very first time they made love, speaking out in response to his questions about what felt good and where, how firm or gentle she liked his touch. And she would reply: there, no, softer, no, more against the bone, yes, kind of in a circle there, right. Honesty about her feelings had characterized Antonia's sexual dynamic with Jonathan from the beginning, and for the three years they lived together.

Then they got married. And immediately, mysteriously, Antonia began holding back small details, tiny fragments of her thoughts and experiences, pieces of sexual knowledge. She began to feel awkward telling him what pleased her. She was a trifle more circumspect: "I was afraid Jonathan would want to know whom I'd done this or that *with*," she says, adding that this was "hard to explain, because he already knew so much about me that it didn't quite make sense for me to withhold *now*." Observing, though, that "he was more uptight about my old boyfriends, and even my former husband, after we married," her new reticence seemed to accommodate his new jealousy perfectly.

> We tried to talk about it—we even called it "marriage-onset weirdness"—but we couldn't locate where it was coming from. But I was always nervous about hurting his feelings, sexually, or making him jealous. I began playing myself down a bit—not seeming too experienced or something. I started lying a little. I did it to make things okay with us, so we could return to our terrific lovemaking. It meant so much to me, and I wanted like hell not to lose it.

Her sudden demureness felt particularly odd since Jonathan already knew about her experiences and her appetite. He had already come to enjoy her "bossiness," as he called it, in bed—as well as her lapses into total passivity. He wasn't aware that he was putting any pressure on her to hold back after they married, and nor was she; she just felt "nervous about hurting his feelings." She'd have the urge to speak, to try new moves, but something stopped her: a strange new shame, a new impulse to be more protective of him, less assertive and lusty than she had been.

Worst of all, she felt less entitled to her fluctuating sexual moods:

> I had tried so hard to learn to speak out for what I wanted— even when what I wanted was no sex for a while. I'd worked hard to overcome my shyness and repression. So when I began falling back into that shyness and repression with the one person I'd conquered it with, well, it was just terrible.

So now she lets Jonathan initiate all experimentation; he's the one who "leads" all the time.

THIS IS THE kind of postmarriage change in mood and behavior that at first had me scratching my head. Two emotionally close sisters reach a conversational stalemate, one hiding from the other her true experience of marriage. A lovely, sociable woman turns distracted and self-conscious after marrying, more alert to unnamed responsibility than to having fun, the caregiver at the party rather than the guest. A sexually sophisticated, mature woman gives up her agency and her voice during sex. But this almost unnoticeable movement away from spontaneity, while interesting to observe, seems almost too unimportant to record, as if so embedded in our understanding of a bride's new role that it's not worth discussing, let alone dissecting. Few of us would question Judy's wifely circumspection, Tracy's nurturing impulse toward her new husband, or Antonia's protective discretion; fewer still would suggest they give up their caring concern.

But as I trace this subtle, progressive diminution of presence, of pleasure, I think of those startling statistics that also defy our understanding. Certain numbers keep haunting me: Depression rates among married women are triple that of their single (never married, divorced, or widowed) female counterparts; severe neurosis among married women is three times that of single women. Here we are thinking that marriage contributes to women's health and well-being, and yet two of the country's most prominent researchers, Myrna Weissman and the late Gerald Klerman, reported almost a decade ago that married women suffer more nervous breakdowns, inertia, loneliness, unhappiness with their looks; more insomnia, heart palpitations, nervousness, and nightmares; more phobias; more feelings of incompetence, guilt, shame, and low self-esteem than single women. After looking carefully at all available data, in fact, they found marriage to be one of only two factors that contribute most to women's depression, the other being low social status.

Married women are far more depressed than married men—in unhappy marriages, three times more; and—interestingly—in happy marriages, five times more. In truth, it is men who are thriving in marriage, now as always, and who show symptoms of psychological and physical distress outside it. Not only their emotional well-being but their very lives, some studies say, depend on being married!

I NOTICED THIS queasy sea change at the altar years ago in the middle of writing a book on adultery, and I began devoting years to exploring what that "something" that happens is. I decided to trace it back to the very beginning of the marriage. And there I stumbled upon the truth of Henry James's observation: "There is a traditional difference between that which people know and that which they agree to admit they know, that which they feel to be a part of life and that which they allow to enter into literature." To which I would add: There's a difference between that which women know and that which the culture is willing to hear. Particularly when it concerns something as treasured as marriage.

And so whatever the "something" is that happens, whether it is unnoticeable or palpable, important or unimportant, a woman stifles her own knowledge, hiding it even from herself, even as she begins to feel, as Judy put it, so "unlike" herself. If not herself, who is she feeling *like*?

KAREN, FORTY-SIX, HAS raised two children, now grown. She is divorced from their father, a man named Calloway, whose name she took when, at nineteen, she eloped with him. They left their Missouri hometown and married in a tiny city hall somewhere in the marshes of Louisiana, having stayed in New Orleans a week longer than they'd planned after the jazz festival, to obtain a license and blood test. She and Calloway support their children equally. Karen, an illustrator, has had fifteen children's books published. She used her name, her maiden name, on all of them, even though Calloway was the name she used for almost twenty years. She has now gone back to her given name fulltime. She even had it changed legally.

So it was a surprise to Karen when her new husband, Sam, automatically used his own last name when introducing her to

friends. Karen felt dissent in the pit of her stomach. She had become quite attached to her own "old" name; it stood for something, the hard-won achievement of knowing who she was, and
she was proud of having gone to the trouble of honoring that
legally. Yet she was unable to say a word of this to her husband.
He'd told her once it would be easier for the neighbors if they
both used the same name, and she had figured she'd deal with
that later, if it came up.

But now "later" is here. And Karen finds it uncomfortable to
go along with "just sort of using his name because it's so much
easier for everyone else to deal with," yet she feels far *more* uncomfortable raising the subject with Sam, or correcting him, or
making "a big deal" of it. "It will be blown up. I feel too old for
this kind of tired issue," she says wearily. "I've thought of many
different ways of handling it—ways that seem completely rational and painless for everyone. But I know Sam. And I know it
would hurt him, whatever way I found to tell him or not tell him
I was going to use my own name. As determined as I once was to
get my name back, I will not risk fighting for it now. I will never
bring it up."

All Karen's rationalizations—that "it's no big thing, anyway,
just a tired old feminist issue"; that "I've found happiness and
I'm not willing to jeopardize it over something as small as this";
even that "if I *really* knew who I was, well, 'What's in a *name?*' as
they say"—do not prevent her stomach from tightening every
time she is called by his name and doesn't speak up about it. She
cannot avoid feeling ashamed of this niggling, insistent self-
betrayal, her conscious, even willing, violation of her own stub-
born wish. She knows her children and her closest friends would
say she's caving in, abandoning herself as she would never

dream of abandoning another. She knows that each time she lets the wrong last name go by, her inaction and her silence "take away a small piece of my self-esteem."

But she's made her decision.

A TALENTED SINGER named Kyra married Doug, a man who had just emerged from a difficult custody battle for his six-year-old daughter, Heather. Doug, who shares custody with Heather's mother, is often away during the weeks that Heather comes to stay with them. Kyra, eager to bond with the child so Doug will be proud—and to provide her new stepdaughter with a stable environment—has given up singing for a while so that, on the weeks when Heather is there, she can be with her. Also, now that she's married and a stepmother, she finds that "my cabaret work feels inappropriate, somehow," a sentiment upsetting to her manager, who is trying to keep booking her once-passionate client, in spite of the singer's sudden disinterest.

Mostly what Kyra worries about is not singing but relation-ships—her and Doug's, her and Heather's, her and Heather's mother's. "She's even worried about *my* relationship with *my* boyfriend now," her manager tells me in front of her. "She keeps saying, 'Hold on to him. You have no idea how important a stable relationship is.' "

"It's true," says Kyra cheerlessly. "I just want everyone to be taken care of. To get along. To be secure. I just want to make sure everyone's safe."

AS I LISTENED to such stories, I was drawn deeper into the mys-tery, more convinced than ever of the need to honor these seemingly slight changes, these charming and considerate ges-tures that would have elicited only approval from onlookers, as significant legs in this journey that is all about reading between the lines, hearing the silences, amplifying tiny signals of distress. Without doing so, I would be left feeling, along with the women, that what was happening was an unlikely story, hardly a story at all.

Could it be that these small erosions of confidence and self-esteem, of independence and resolve, apparently brought on only by caring—nothing obvious, nothing soul-killing—might contribute somehow to an explanation for those statistics we know but don't understand? One fact about our nation's astronomical divorce rate, which is the highest on the planet and rising, is this: Our divorces occur early in a marriage, on average, four to seven years after the wedding, most frequently even earlier, between two to four years. Young people are especially divorce-prone: 42 percent of those divorced in 1988, for instance, were twenty-five to thirty-four.

When I ask the women what they think is going on, they feel caught between expressing distress and expressing their gratitude for being married. To bring up the darker side of their postwedding experience seems to call into question their own normality, even their capacity for happiness. Since the joy of the wedding and its aftermath are—in the myth we were raised on—indisputable, any unwelcome or uncomfortable feelings simply make no sense. How can a woman be discontented when she's just taken on the very role she's longed for most?

When Judy noticed something was different when she married, she asked her married friends, "Is the first year always like this?" She heard an astonishing number of embarrassed yeses, followed by a standard explanation that tries to make sense of that answer—tries, in fact, to make this traitorous discomfort sound inevitable. She heard the adjustment theory, which explains her condition as either the natural letdown from the euphoria of being a bride or the unavoidable friction of two people who, like two emery boards, rub against each other till their edges are worn smooth. But she and Jack had already lived together for three years before they got married! So it was only marriage, not each other, to which they apparently needed to adjust. Trying to understand her own feelings in the context of wedded happiness and well-being only confuses her and fills her with self-doubt. So rather than face the terrifying questions "What's the matter with me?" and "What do I do now?" she decides "it" will pass; "it" is nothing. "It" is what they mean by "compromise," and she'll get used to it. Her displeasure is hormonal, maybe. She's fine. She'll get over it. She will, as they all promise, "adjust."

I've noticed that wives often bury their anxiety in some variation of this adjustment theory, rather than investigate what they really feel or doubt the institution of marriage itself. Perhaps any questions they might have about marriage threaten to evoke Freud's famous question, "What do women want?" And women detect the exasperation in it, an impatience suggesting that whatever they have should be enough. They sense it isn't a sincere question but a veiled criticism: If *this* isn't what you want, then what on earth *is*?" And they feel stranded.

And yet women will speak up when they sense a sincere desire for an answer—from them. When a chapter of my last book called "The Perfect Wife" was excerpted in the June 1992 issue of *McCall's* magazine, the editors invited women across the country to think about their own marriages and respond to the query "Do you feel you gave up part of your true self?" Hundreds of letters from readers poured in saying that indeed they did.

Two years later, in an infidelity survey in *New Woman* magazine, 83 percent of the respondents said they believed that "wives submerge a vital part of themselves" when they marry.

And in a survey conducted two years later by *New Woman*'s senior editor, Stephanie von Hirschberg, and me, we asked the readership, younger and more openly sexual than readers of *McCall's,* if they felt they had lost themselves in any way when they married. Of the five thousand women who responded, more than two thousand attached additional pages to their survey forms, so that they could say in their own words, often at length, how they felt altered at the altar.

Some of the women you meet in this book will be those I met and interviewed as a result of these letters; others come from a wider net I've cast over the years. One might think that these responses would be from women who are not doing well in their marriages—but that's not at all the case. They weren't writing in to complain. They were saying something vastly different and new—that soon after marriage, they had fallen under a kind of spell—and it is this odd, surprising enchantment I am tracking in this book.

Does this happen to all women at marriage? No, but to enough of them, even right here in these letters, to be alarming—a sufficient number to make it impossible for me to complete in-depth interviews with even these.

These are mostly middle-class women, for it is they and their marriages I am interested in, because they are most vulnerable to the particular process I'm charting—for reasons that will become clearer in Chapter Three.

I want to emphasize that I'm not a social scientist and this is not a "random" sample or a scientific study. My results are not analyzed by computer, but by me. However, I believe that interviewing women over time and in-depth—and in private, which random sampling can prohibit—has allowed me to find out far more than I might have from any questionnaire, or indeed any other method I can think of, and that my thesis, arising as it does from an intimacy and trust built over time and deep involvement, could not have emerged otherwise. I hope these questions I raise in this book, so riveting for me and resonant for thousands of women, will be studied further.

In looking at women who, like Antonia, feel the impulse to hide their sexual experience and agency and voice at marriage, would we find clues to the half-joking question that regularly appears on the covers of magazines and books, "Is there sex after marriage?" In these ordinary stories of sexual subterfuge in the name of kindness, of sexual histories rewritten, can we find in marriage new rules in couples' sex play, new and hidden principles governing erotic desire?

If we're really concerned about the mystery of why traditional signs of marital dissatisfaction—sometimes adultery, sometimes depression, sometimes divorce—now occur so early, wouldn't we insist on looking more closely at the microscopic clues in these couples' sexual lives?

If we really care to understand why up to 65 percent of all new marriages end, and most of them after only a few years, wouldn't we spotlight the most surprising statistic of all: that whereas in 1970 most divorces were the man's idea, today, 60 to 75 percent of divorces are initiated by *women*?

A WOMAN'S PRESENT behavior isn't all that changes once she crosses the threshold of marriage. Even her past behavior gets a retroactive makeover. The women I spoke with, whether in their twenties or their sixties, began revising their previous, premarriage lives as soon as the ring was on their finger. No sooner were the wedding photos taken than they began to alter the picture of who they were before marriage, as if to shutter up a building before gutting it. Burning old love letters is a premarriage ritual that many of these women confessed to. Yet it was a ritual that felt neither destructive nor dangerous, but rather protective and loving: They believed they were welcoming marriage in by saying good-bye to the past.

But their good-byes sounded suspiciously like "good riddance." *This* past—a modern woman's years of single, sexual, autonomous living—seems to need to be not just lovingly released but brusquely jettisoned at the altar. Ordinarily, memory accompanies us into the future; our present sense of self is rooted in the rich mulch of our experience, and we treasure our memories for the very continuity and self-definition they offer, for their power to hold us together across the chasms of change. But at marriage something extraordinary happens to a woman. She decides that a substantial chunk of her history is unwelcome and has to be cast off, as if it were a spent but still radioactive first-stage rocket that must not be allowed to accompany her into the perfect orbit of married life.

TAMI, A COOK at an organic restaurant in Connecticut, tells me she stopped writing in her daily journal the day she got married eighteen years ago. The diary "was my confidante," she says. "I put in everything." She was an idealistic young woman, she says, afraid of nothing except "sinking into mediocrity," and her journal reflected that passion. She doesn't know why she stopped writing in it, exactly, except that she felt that when she married she "had a different identity." Her husband urged her to continue, but she didn't, couldn't. "I did try again," she says. "When I felt like having my old body back, and an old friend back, when I had to burst out, to tell somebody something." But it didn't take. Her husband "wants me back the way I was," complete with passion, idealism, the daily journal. She doesn't know what it is—"the kids, or me, or what"—but she can't get it, or that woman, back.

SARAH, A TWENTY-NINE-YEAR-OLD social worker married less than a year, says she feels "stupid" when she talks about the turbulence of her former relationships.

"Stupid?" I ask. "How?"

"Stupid because it was all so fraught. Everything was so *intense,* so meaningful all the time."

"What was stupid about it, if it was meaningful?"

"All those relationships feel now just like so much wasted time, so many wasted emotions spent on all these men I don't *remember* anymore," Sarah says. "And even if I could, and I liked them, I couldn't see them for dinner, even if I wanted to—right? because you *can't.*" And so a whole vibrant history of sex and intensity, joy and rage and agony gets bleached out and shrunken down to little more than a prologue to marriage, an opening act for the main attraction, a tryout for "the real thing." Or highlights—like Tami's or Sarah's Greatest Hits—summed up and recorded on a single disc. Married men remember, even idealize, their bachelor past as their "glory days," as "freedom"; married women often remember their past as fleeting and unimportant. There is irony here, and delusion, for the happily-ever-after expectations that even the most sophisticated women still bring to marriage—that its intimacy will somehow be more sublime, its emotions safer, surer, purer, realer, and certainly less harrowing—are, in fact, the *un*real thing, different from the relationships they know. We are now entering an ideal, and our vast experience of real relationships is seen as irrelevant and inferior to it; inappropriate, even inimical, rather than helpful. So we "disappear" it.

There's a way in which these stories, even as they gather momentum, still elicit in me that same dismissive response I saw in the women I spoke with—that they're minor and momentary, not sufficient evidence, too subtle for significance, rather than the tip of some larger, momentous iceberg. Surely, whether a woman stops writing in her journal, dissembles about the number of boyfriends she's had, or stops dancing to rock-and-roll bands isn't what's driving her to divorce court.

Or is it?

Why *are* marriages dissolving so early and so quickly? I know all the theories: moral decay, narcissism, feminism, the sexual revolution, mothers working outside the home, mothers staying at home, single mothers, deadbeat dads, the decline of the work ethic, the Pill, premarital sex, the decline of religious training, overall permissiveness, a decline in "family values." Without these impediments, the thinking goes, marriage would be ideal again, the way it used to be in the good old days when there was no question how long a marriage lasted and when Mom and Dad and the kids had the right values.

And then I see how much couples care about their marriages. How hard they're willing to work on their relationships, how deeply, profoundly concerned they are, how sensitive to their new spouses, how eager to have a good marriage! And I see all the work these women are doing, emotional work of which these little behavior shifts are a piece, work that men are either not doing in the same way or are oblivious to, or expect, or *don't* expect, and I remember that yes, these many small self-sacrifices, these expectations that we play out so reflexively, *are* crucial, far more relevant to the survival of marriage, perhaps, than some of the bigger, more obvious and workable issues. They just take a little more time—and courage, maybe—to understand.

Intertwined with the new wife's impulse to cast off her sexually autonomous past is the inclination to hide it from her husband, to protect him from knowledge of the unruly, unwifely woman she used to be, even when that is the woman he fell in love with. Certainly one major motive, admitted or not, for destroying old diaries and letters is the fear that the husband might find them, and find out . . . what? What doesn't he already know—and love? Isn't this the man she's supposed to be letting into her innermost heart and soul? And doesn't *he* have a sexual past, as rich and tumultuous as hers?

Bettina talks about her terror of "arousing my husband's jealousy. I couldn't stand talking about stuff I did sexually and then hearing the questions: Who did you do *that* with? I didn't know you'd gone *that* far."

Protecting her husband from hurt or jealousy is a key motive for a woman's self-revision, but she is protecting herself as well: from being revealed in some imagined unlovely light, as too experienced, too knowledgeable, too sexual, too problematic, too hungry or insatiable, too *something*. The healthy pleasure-seeking that all the magazines urge on the independent young woman seems suddenly not so appealing in a wife. Many women hide from their husbands the better part of their sexual history, slashing the number and importance of the men they've been involved with, editing not only what they did and with whom, but entire chapters, whole human beings, right along with what they felt, as if the unexpurgated version had the power to ruin their lives. "Jim? Oh, right, that guy I dated for a little while." This was the response of Jean, age forty-one, when her husband asked about a man who had been, in fact, very important to her. Alison, thirty-three, hid from her husband the existence of a man she had slept with strictly for sex. "I don't know if I wanted to seem as if I didn't just have sex without love, or whether I wanted to seem as if I wasn't that sexually driven," she says. Greta, fifty when she married for the second time, found herself referring to all her pleasurable adventures as if they had costarred her former husband, Henry, when in fact many of them had taken place in casual or short-term relationships.

I seemed too experienced, somehow, too promiscuous. Now, that is far from the reality, given that I was single for almost twenty years, and I began having sex late—at about nineteen. But you just don't talk about, let alone recall lovingly, your thirteen sexual partners before your first marriage and your six partners or whatever after your divorce. It sounds unseemly. So I lumped them all together. I was both implying that I hadn't slept with anyone but my first husband and legitimizing my behavior, like sex is only legitimate in marriage. I still don't know what or who I did it for.

Like throwing out old love letters, cleaning up one's sexual résumé is "something women just do." But they don't just do it any old time; they do it when they marry. Freud spoke of this impulse toward what I call "retroactive monogamy" as "the demand that the girl shall bring with her into marriage with one man no memory of sexual relations with another." He saw it as "nothing but a logical consequence of the exclusive right of possession over a woman which is the essence of monogamy—it is but an extension of this monopoly on to the past." And bizarrely, wives' collusive impulse for a major cover-up seems to click in automatically even when, like Antonia, a woman has been living with the same man for years and has been quite free and frank with him.

When a boyfriend becomes a husband, women suddenly feel compelled to start speaking in another voice, not their own: the voice of a wife. They can have a strong, irrational sense that their former selves are no longer relevant, somehow seditious; and little by little those selves, with their hard-won wealth of knowledge, experience, and pleasure, are driven underground, hushed like the existence of an illegitimate child. In their place, women present a weirdly whitewashed version of themselves, one that better fits what they sense they now "should" be and "should" desire. Trading in the real-life past for a more perfect version—less seasoned, less sexual—they nevertheless do not feel they are doing any harm to themselves or to their relationships. The urge to censor the record feels benign, even when their husbands observe and question the censorship and lament it: After all, wives feel they are doing it "for" the marriage. Sealing up the seething, living past seems a small price to pay for the fulfillment and renewal we have been promised as married women.

WHY DOES JUDY feel caught, unable to articulate her distress even with her sister, even with herself? Why has Tracy changed from a woman who has a wonderful time dancing at a Christmas party into one who worries about her husband's food and drink intake? Why has she metamorphosed from a "sexy" dresser into a modest one—without even noticing?

Why has Kyra stopped singing, as if responding to some cue about wives and *relationships,* now that she has a lawful permanent one?

Why does Karen feel embarrassed fighting for her own name, as if it were threatening, hurtful to do so? Why does Antonia feel the need to censor her sexual history and conceal her sexual desires now—only now—that the man she loves has become her husband?

This is not the 1950s; this is not the "problem with no name" that Betty Friedan named "the feminine mystique." These are women with freedom and jobs, with everything they hoped for.

What has happened? What do they mean, these stealthy, creeping impulses to wear different clothes, to change focus, and names and hairstyles, and rules and habits that once meant so much? What is it about wives' compulsion to withhold information, monitor their behavior, cover their emotions, suppress questions, shift concerns, take on extraordinary new responsibility, to hide so many vital parts of themselves from the men they love so much—and then to dismiss that missing vitality as "irrelevant"? Why are these changes happening at this particular juncture, *when they become wives*—and not before, when they were dating or living with a man—often the same man? Why now, in the midst of the very love they have been waiting for, the sanctified love in which true trust, sexuality, intimacy, and authenticity are at last supposed to blossom? How does a woman come to sense that, like a body too unruly, fleshy, and desirous for a petite size 8 dress, her real life does not quite fit into the story she has just entered?

Why is it irrelevant whether the bride is in her twenties, as Sarah, Kyra, and Tracy are; in her thirties, as Judy and Alison are; in her forties, as Tami and Karen are; or in her fifties, as Antonia and Greta are?

What is it that makes women no longer quite "themselves" and so in some crucial way not even fully present *in* the relationships that they once so comfortably and happily inhabited?

As I thought about these questions, I remembered those depression and divorce statistics—how they implicate marriage as a dwelling quite different from what we've believed, that is, women's natural and nourishing element, an environment in which women thrive and flourish. And I realized that here, surrounding me, fleshing out these statistics, are thousands of letters from women who have written me on their own and who responded to those surveys I mentioned, women who said they had modified their words and their voices, their looks, their dress, their mannerisms, their entire self-presentation when they married. Here, in the cartons of letters I keep sifting through, readers—with no incentive to fill out a questionnaire beyond expressing themselves and helping me gather material for this book—said they became less playful, less flirtatious, less ambitious, less assertive, less sexual, less open, and less honest with their partners, their families, their friends, and themselves. At the moment of marriage—the happiest day of many of these women's lives—they unwittingly gave up much of what they enjoyed, and enjoyed about themselves, as well as what their husbands enjoyed about them, in order to aspire to a more conventional, more conforming, more proper and modest and toned-down version of themselves called a "wife."

How Victorian this all sounds, so old-fashioned! Who *is* that masked woman, the wife, and what could possibly make her behave so differently from the single or divorced woman she was only moments before? Who is this "other woman" she thinks she should be, and what is the voice that commands her?

2
—

The Witness

Who are you, whose speech
sounds far out of reach?

—W. H. Auden
"The Witness"

THESE SLIGHT ALTERATIONS in communication, along with almost imperceptible shifts in concern, behavior, and attitude,
mark the beginning of an intricate process that unfolds slowly,
subtly, and incrementally for many a new wife. Her change in
status, both legal and social, has changed her, of course, but in
ways she couldn't have imagined or foreseen. A new emphasis—
another way of seeing herself and her marriage—seems to encourage her to view both from the outside, a position that
conflicts with the experience from within. She now seems to be
juggling two stories about love, each relating her world, her life,
and *her* from a different point of view.

She responds carefully, with just the slightest change in what
she says or withholds, what she presents and what she covers up,
and how she feels about herself—until finally she senses a gap

between who she was before she married and who she is supposed to become as a wife. And the gap, like train tracks diverg-
ing, widens as she goes along until she suddenly finds herself
miles off course. She discovers she's on an entirely different tra-
jectory from the one she sighted down for herself.

It begins when a "should" voice enters a wife's head. What a
shock to see how quickly after the wedding "I do" translates into
"I should"! Tracy, twenty-six when she married Tom, only half-
facetiously itemized for me the things she "ought" to be doing
and feeling and becoming, a list that was her guide through the
early days of her new life: She should be thinner. She should be
sexier. She should want sex more. She should want sex *less*. She
should be making more money. She should stay home. She
should be thinking about having a child. She should be focusing
on her career. She should be focusing on her husband's career.
She should entertain her husband's friends more. She should
see her own friends more. Or less. Or on weekdays only, when
they won't "interfere" with her marriage. She should be happier. Kinder. Neater. More productive. More cheerful. More
grateful. More frugal. In a better mood. Nicer to her mother.
Nicer to *his* mother. She should be giving more to *charity*.

Tracy is amused by the contradictions in this list, by how
many opposites she feels she should be enacting at once. She
wonders where this arduous inventory comes from, how she
herself got hold of it, what all those "shoulds" are driving at.
Whom do they describe? What do they prescribe? It's not her
husband who presented this odd wish list to her, nor is it her
mother or father, yet she didn't dream it up. Who is this perfect
woman this new wife thinks she should become? What story is
being told to her? Who is whispering instructions about "earn-

ing" love in her ear, becoming *better,* and why does she feel so helpless to resist them?

Certainly she understands that this idealized wife is not anyone she resembles or would even want to be? Tracy can't quite picture this overachieving whirlwind, suspects that no one like her ever existed; yet somewhere in some remote region of her brain is the haunting presence of such a woman. Tracy resists her own compulsion to try to become her, knowing both that it is impossible and unhealthy and that she doesn't even want to.

Nevertheless, here is this anachronistic, unreal model of womanhood that has materialized along with her wedding ring, has moved into her own home uninvited, a tireless icon who is relaxed, sexually eager but not *too,* easily satisfied, contented and undemanding, attractive yet modest, nurturing and giving and caring, like the memory of some long-lost angel.

Tracy mocks herself for taking such a ridiculous list to heart, yet she—and virtually every one of the women I spoke with— confessed to the conviction that if they did not adhere to this internalized catalog of cultural expectations, they might jeopardize their marriages and lose the approval of their friends and family. They would feel like failures, like "bad" wives, even as they knew this was, as Tracy said, "insane." The icon might be ridiculed, the effort to become her impossible, but few women I've spoken with are unaware of her image; fewer still have been able to resist the pressure to try to acquire at least some of her famous domestic graces and virtues.

Adrienne, a New York art historian, remembers becoming this icon "within a year of marrying my first husband," from whom she is now long divorced. She says the minute she married she thought, "What do I do now? I know, I'll *cook!*"

I had learned what was expected of me. I don't think it was he who told me, I just knew. I didn't want to go along with it, but I did, because I knew that I couldn't be a wife and still be really, really me. After a year and a half, my plans for my life, my own needs, had disappeared, since I had formed them around my doctor husband's so neatly that I no longer resembled the woman I was before I got married. Just eighteen months before, I had been a singer, an artist, a woman with plans. Now I became a little blurred about those plans and very quickly dropped them. It wasn't that I announced it or even noticed it; they were just no longer there, no longer spoken about, put on hold until—what? I don't know.

Adrienne's atavistic understanding that her first moves as a wife usher her into a specific story, initiate her into a behavior appropriate to the protagonist of that story, is both laughably familiar and terrifyingly unfamiliar. It means, she says, "that at the very least I was feeling under some kind of pressure to be different from who I was. Different from who I really am. That it was time to follow, I don't know, a whole new script."

This pressure on our bride compelling her to "follow a whole new script" about who she "should" be, how she "should" behave to be loved, even how she "should" feel in the relationship confuses her. Her own voice, after all, speaks directly from her gut, draws from her own experience, observation, and knowledge, expresses her needs and desires. It alerts her: "I want, I feel, I know, I think." Because this grounded, embodied voice communicates her genuine feelings, her self, it is comforting, true, and honest; it feels right. From such a solid position of authority

and strength, her own real voice promises not perfect harmony
with another person but authentic contact and, when answered
by that other person's voice, connection—"relationship"—that
experience that means so much to her.

This pressure—sometimes a voice, sometimes an urge, sometimes an internal coercion—catches her by surprise. It seems to
have been there from the moment the word *marriage* became
a fact, sometimes arriving right at the altar, like the witness
required at every wedding to authorize the marriage certificate.
It seems to be overseeing her actions and monitoring her
thoughts and plans from her wedding day on, advising her,
promising—but only if she heeds its advice—the loving relationship with her husband that she wants. Yet responding to this
witness, she begins to act out something vastly different from
what she instinctively knows about how to connect with others.
Rather than living an expansive story of love, she lives a con-
strained one, static, like a cautionary tale. The narrator seems to
be coming from inside her, yet its words are someone else's; its
authority is intrusive, dicomfiting, and scary. "Don't," it implies.
"Don't do that, or you'll lose your love."

Whose voice is this? Her husband's? Sometimes it seems to be,
but would the man she lived with take such an authoritarian, censorious position with her all of a sudden? And would she be so ex-
cruciatingly hypersensitive to a voice that had never before been
harshly critical and controlling? Would she have wed such a man?

Yet the voice of what I call the Witness is so compelling, so
sure in its knowledge, so clear about how to have a relationship,
about what you do and how it's supposed to happen and what
such a union looks like from the outside, that soon she comes to

doubt what she knew and felt and to edit and even ignore her own voice. Once alerted to the Witness's vision of how things should be, she starts viewing her relationship and marriage accordingly, assessing it from this external vantage point, rather than from her own. Appearances suddenly mean more than they did. As she begins to revise her voice to jibe with what the Witness tells her she should be saying, doing, thinking, even wanting, she begins to hand over to it her sense of how to *be* in marriage, as if she knows nothing about relationships at all. She awaits further instructions.

She has an image of an ideal relationship and just how it should proceed, a dream that bullies its way into her waking reality. She knows it is a myth, all of it, from the virginal white wedding dress straight through to happily ever after, yet she begins to insist on it, suddenly and inexplicably fearful that something is amiss or that she will feel cheated should she fail to experience even a moment of it. Novelist Jill Eisenstadt writes of worrying, on her wedding night, that guests would stay beyond dawn, making it impossible for her and her husband to consummate their wedding vows. She had had sex with him before, she notes in "The Virgin Bride," *The New York Times,* June 16, 1996, and yet

it was our wedding night. Of course we'd have sex. This I truly believed despite the hour. Blame it on bridal magazines, Hollywood or my own naivete, but when I agreed to take part in the marriage rites I assumed that meant all of them. Why else would I have worn the white gown or the garter that gave me prickly heat? Held up the ceremony to shove something blue (a Canada Dry label) into my cleavage? Allowed my dad to give

me away? Maybe it was unrealistic to expect a bubble bath or-
gasmathon. But surely our vows would be consummated. For
all I knew, our license wasn't even valid otherwise; unravished
come sunrise, I'd turn into a pumpkin, or worse—a single girl
again.

They did not have sex that night. Which prompted Eisenstadt
to conduct her own unscientific survey of other couple's wedding nights, at which point she discovered that twenty out of the
twenty-five couples she asked hadn't consummated their vows
on the big night, either. "Laugh we might, but deep down we
still feel we're just supposed to have sex on our wedding nights.
It's not rational, it's ritual."

That ritual has a way of striking the rational dumb is evi-
denced by the way Eisenstadt felt the next day when, fully
dressed and reflecting on the dismal omission the night before,
she wondered: "Was the marriage off to a bad start? Were we
doomed to a future of pecklike kisses? Fluorescent-light din-
ners? Twin beds? . . . What if we never had sex again?"

And this rumination is just what the Witness intends when it
urges a wife to hew to ritual and, for whatever reasons, she does
not.

Just as the Witness notifies women how things are supposed to
be, so it tells them how they are supposed to be. And it can be
disarming when it pipes up.

A writer named Joan, whose first husband died some years
ago, is only half joking when she offers her reason for not re-
marrying: "I'd have to cook him *lunch,*" she says to me in front
of the man she adores, the man whose lunch is in question. "You

don't make me lunch now," he says gently, "so why on earth would you have to if we married?"

"I just would," she says, and she is very serious.

TRACY, MEANWHILE, INCREASINGLY upset by the subtle, insidious infiltration of these strict warnings into her married life, begins to investigate its origins.

She cannot help ascribing it to Tom: His expectations of her seem to have changed, after all, along with her own of herself. Now he assumes she'll be home at a certain time, and that she'll be planning if not preparing their meals. And yet Tom himself is puzzled by his own husbandly expectations and unwilling to let Tracy dwindle into a Wife. *He's* the one who protested when she gave away her leather skirt, he reminds her; *he's* the one who urged to her to dance and have fun at the Christmas party; *he's* the one who supports—sometimes more than Tracy herself does—her unconventional, fun-loving, sexy spirit, encouraging her to keep it. And yet now he also wants dinner on the table! It's as if there are two voices in him, too. And this other one has a booming, hollow authority that takes him by surprise as much as it does her—an authority he doesn't question. Clearly, what this voice wants for Tom isn't necessarily what Tom wants—any more than it's what his wife wants. So while sometimes this voice seems to speak through him, it's somehow not his voice. And, as to Tracy's reaction to it, they both observe that when it speaks through him it scares her more than Tom's own familiar voice used to, even when they were fighting, before marriage—as if it's finding her out, calling her on something terrible she's done.

What's more, she hears it even when it's not coming from him!

Is it, then, her conscience? Her mother's voice? Her father's? Her first-grade teacher's? *God's?* "I went back to my Presbyterian roots, to my childhood, to see where this dreamy scene of marriage came from, and this good-wife role I was sleepwalking through. Was it buried in the hymns I sang as a child? I checked out the hymnal. Nothing. There's always the shadow of somebody's good behavior in hymns, I've noticed, but it's usually *Jesus'* good behavior." She was stumped.

If she can't figure out whose voice it is, at least she knows *when* she began to hear it. It was even before the Christmas dance,

right after we married. So we're at this dinner party, and Joe, a friend, tells a really stupid dirty joke that's going around— one of those jokes where the genie gives you whatever wish you want and this one guy asks for a big penis and gets a big piano—something like that, and I think it's really funny and goofy, but you know what? I feel inhibited. I find myself smacking Tom on the arm when he laughs, like some terrible *good woman* who's monitoring the jokes tonight and isn't sure the word *penis* should be uttered in her company. So what comes out of my mouth? *"Oh, that's terrible, Joe!"* and I lower my eyes and laugh just a tiny bit, as if I were not supposed to be amused by such filth, as if I would be thought less of if I did, *as if the joke were unfit for a wife.*

Tracy remembers how she felt the next day:

It was very, very disturbing to me. Because I saw that I knew how to *do* this woman, to play her. The Virgin Schoolmarm Wife Madonna. We could now be divided, Tom and me, into bad boy and good girl and nobody would ever notice except me. And I thought to myself, I may hate her, but here I am acting her out faster than I can act out me. Now, that's scary. Funny or not, her personality is more compelling than mine, somehow. What's truly awful about it is that by the time you've done it once or twice—you know, slapped your husband's arm and said, "Oh, honey, how *could* you!" or pulled away that piece of chocolate cake or that beer because you know he's dieting, the role starts to come frighteningly easily. You become that most amazing thing, the overseer. The arbiter. The person who will declare what is and what is not fit material to present or to eat or to say in polite company. The one who will laugh reluctantly at the joke but make it clear that that joke really "shouldn't" be laughed at.

Elaine, forty, says she came under the guidance of the Witness from the day she got married at age thirty-two. In our conversations, she tried hard to locate that moment when she first altered her normal behavior even slightly, when she covered over a word or a thought somewhat, adjusted an observation, an opinion, a feeling, or a demand, spoke in a more moderated voice or made a more giving, compliant, or censorious move:

It was the night after we got married. We had had a fight, our first since the stupid stuff before and about the wedding. I suddenly understood that I had better fix the fight, that it was my responsibility, and that I was sort of better at doing that, moving us toward not fighting. I understood that I was the relationship pro. That it was "our" marriage but my emotional responsibility. I was the one who would end the fight, manage the emotional stuff, keep the marriage on an even keel. I felt a little funny about it, since I hadn't felt that before with Jack, but I also felt okay about it, like it was my job and I'd do it well. I was the one who was better at relationships, so my new position sort of codified that responsibility, if you see what I mean.

In becoming the "relationship pro," Elaine began to modify her usual response in an argument, opting for a more careful version of herself, choosing a moderate, conciliatory tone she dubs "more wifely." This voice is one that above all "did not interfere with conversation," did not censor her husband's voice, even if it meant censoring her own. She did not cry, shout, or emote openly as she once might have; she began to alter the volume and tone of her voice, to make it sound lower, "more reassuring." Elaine says, "I wanted to show that I was reasonable, rather than emotional, and that we could get through what might be an endless fight just by my being understanding enough to accommodate his feelings and my own. I thought if I screamed—I used to, you know—I would undermine what I was trying to do here. You can't be angry, I kept saying to myself. He won't listen if you are."

"Had he listened to you before when you were angry?" I ask.

"Yes," she says.

"And what were you trying to do now?"

"At the time, I would have said that I was trying to be more mature, like I thought married people were supposed to be. That I was learning how to fight in an adult way. A kind of play-acting that I thought was grown up, more like the fair fighting we should do as married people. And to prove I wasn't a shrew."

I ask her how she defines "shrew," and she laughs.

"Someone who screams. Who is unreasonable. Who orders her husband around. Who doesn't work to end arguments. Who is *angry*. A bitch."

"And who must be tamed?"

"Yeah."

THE GOOD WIFE, the attractive, feminine wife, Elaine feels, is "neither angry nor emotional." She loses her very goodness, attractiveness, and femininity when her voice no longer pleases others, when it rises and falls, intensifies and vocalizes strong feeling—need, desire, anger. Once that voice is heard, particularly if it is an unmelodious, dissonant voice and bursts out in the middle of a fight, she is called "strident" or "shrill," a "shrew" and a "bitch."

We both notice that there are no similar terms for a husband's voice—the pejorative "strident" and "shrill" are reserved for women. Men's authoritative, urgent, loud, angry, or hostile voices are not given negative labels because men are supposed to be in authority and are not obliged to speak in hushed tones to disguise or suppress strong, passionate feelings. There are few disparaging words for a loud and angry man himself—nothing quite so demeaning as "bitch," for example—for the simple reason that men, married or not, are not obliged to please (either by the register of their voices or by what they say). They have other cultural demons, but not ones specifically inhibiting the expression of their needs, desires, and anger. In fact, they are expected to voice them and act on them; there is no public censure of their masculinity when they do.

Men are not asked to monitor others' jokes, opinions, or behavior; to "tame," "socialize," or "reform" them. Husbands, then, do not hear these particular "shoulds" informing *them* about new ways to behave, speak, think, and feel after marriage—customs designed to please others and to earn love and approval. No, men do not hear much from the Witness; like the

serpent in the garden, it speaks only to women. Men are sometimes the channels for its voice, but very rarely the targets.
There are enormous cultural expectations of husbands, of
course—providing for and protecting their families among
them—but in one crucial way these differ from those of wives:
Men rarely confuse the "shoulds" of their role with their own
needs, desires, or character. So while men may appreciate the
value of selflessness, no one expects them to be innately, bio-
logically self-sacrificing, as if any other impulse were a violation
of their very nature. By contrast, women's "inborn" selflessness
is so expected it's even scorned, as Somerset Maugham illus-
trated when he remarked, "A woman will always sacrifice herself
if you give her the opportunity. It's her favorite form of self-
indulgence."

"Self-indulgence" is hardly the way most women would describe it. We know from studies that women, in order to stay connected to those they love, will readily name themselves the
guardians of relationships and feel responsible for others' well-
being. Our sense of self and our self-esteem depend upon how
well we feel we are doing this, our job.

At the time, Tracy thought she was doing her job—keeping
her relationship strong—when she jabbed her husband in the
middle of a dirty joke, and "absentmindedly" took his drink
away from him at the Christmas party. Elaine, too, experienced
her decision to keep her voice down in an argument, to be the
arbiter, the guarantor of marital harmony, as a choice made for
the benefit of her relationship, an ancient and accepted benign
reorientation, even a welcome rite of passage into the long-
anticipated role of wife.

Greeting her there in her new role is this compelling Witness

to her transformation from woman to wife. In urging her not to
be herself when she enters marriage but to change herself into
a person more worthy of the true love marriage promises, the
Witness gives specific instructions about how to sound and look
and be, even how to feel and what to desire, in order to receive
the love she so wants and have the relationship she has dreamed
of. Because she loves her husband and wants his love so much,
because she names herself the guardian of their relationship,
because she sees these instructions as the route to intimacy; because she sees marriage as renewal; for all these reasons, she will
take to heart the coaching of the Witness and try earnestly to follow its instructions.

She may make a few feeble attempts to resist; after all, the ways
she feels pressed to behave are so new, so unfamiliar, so different from how she acted before she got married. So much seems
to depend, in this new story, on her and her alone! So much
feels disconnected from her past experience! If the Witness is
really so concerned with her and her marriage, she may wonder,
why does it disregard her feelings so? Why does it judge and ob-
jectify her, rather than sympathize? Why doesn't it affirm all she
has learned over the years about loving and living with people?

Why is this foreign, unfamiliar Witness vying so with her own
voice and experience?

THE SINGLE WOMEN I've talked with over the past decade, particularly during the seven years I wrote a sex-and-relationship
column in *Mademoiselle,* are far less inclined to hear a condemning "should" voice, and even less inclined, if they hear one, to
heed it. This is not to say there isn't a kind of collective societal
etiquette or script for unmarried women regarding the art of

winning men, but today's single women feel emboldened to disregard such old-fashioned advice and to honor instead their
own embodied voices—until the desire or pressure to get married overwhelms them. Until then, though, with support from
their friends, their families, and their therapists, many single
women now feel authorized to pay attention to their own needs
and desires, to fight for their rights at work and in love, to insist
that their selves not get lost in their relationships and that their
voices be heard. They are aware of the omnipresent pressure to
fix themselves to fit into relationships, and they gather with
friends to try instead to fix relationships to fit *them*. Anne, now
forty-five, tells me how careful she was on her own and her
friends' behalf while she was single:

> It would have been so impossible for someone to have been
> so controlling [as this voice] before I was married. I would
> have heard it; I would have been alert to it, rejected it. Nobody
> pushed me around when I was single; and if anyone tried to, I
> talked to my friends about it and *they* gave me the courage to
> push back when I made too many concessions to a boss or a
> boyfriend or my family. At that time I had an entire army of
> women behind me, warning me against the ways we all tend to
> go under in relationships, to lose our bearings and our self-
> esteem. I didn't want, above all else, to be a victim. Those
> women are gone now. They do not know how to negotiate this
> new terrain called "marriage"—they wouldn't presume to
> back me up the way they did before.

This makes Anne feel she is betraying those who were keeping her from betraying herself.

So now I find myself doing things I say are "for the relationship" that I would never dare tell my friends about. They
would be horrified at how much I do in order to keep this
thing going. And I am ashamed at the way I now make all these
weird concessions. I don't know if I'm just afraid of being seen
as a victim or if I've genuinely renounced something strong in
me that I feel slipping away. But I know I'm giving up something I don't want to admit to—something I pretend is "compromise" but that most emphatically isn't. Compromise I'd be
proud of. This is . . . renouncing something. And I can't say
anything to my husband, because I don't quite know what it is.
Like, "Honey, I feel I'm giving up too much for our marriage"?
He'd be flabbergasted.

Out of embarrassment, she says nothing to her friends:

I can just hear them saying, "I can't believe what a *wuss* you've
turned into. God, Anne, *you've really changed* . . ."

So now she has twice kept silent, once about her true feelings,
then about her sorrow at having withheld them. She feels she
has "renounced" a very personal authority she valued and
shared with her friends, her own brand of feminism that she and
her women friends fought for: What she now senses she must do
to have a married relationship exceeds what she would have allowed herself in any relationship before. And she feels a kind of
shame. "Look, I had these happily-ever-after expectations like
everyone else. And I knew that some of it was possible and most
of it wasn't."
But she observes that while she now has everything she has

ever wanted, she nevertheless, oddly, does not feel what she is supposed to feel about having them. The story she is living feels more static than she expected, and she, in it, duller somehow.

And she feels twice ashamed. She knows neither how to challenge the Witness nor exactly how to resist it. She doesn't know whom to complain to about the fact that she tends to heed its words, for she senses that heeding them is unquestionably the proper thing to do. She doesn't know in whom to confide that she hears this voice in the first place. Like Anne and Elaine, Tracy, and Judy, she feels like a misfit in this new world of marriage, an outsider, feels that in fact she *needs* a guide—the way new mothers felt back in the 1960s and 1970s when, swamped with the medical profession's often counterintuitive advice on proper mothering, they nevertheless came to think they couldn't raise their babies without it. She feels, moreover, something more subversive: that she might not be the kind of woman who has it in her to make a good wife, that she's doing it all wrong, somehow. She feels as if to mention these feelings aloud—I don't like this! This feels weird!—is dangerous, even ungrateful, "like, here I am with a wonderful husband and I'm so happy and I've finally got everything I ever wanted and so what's my problem?" She is hardly aware of this feeling before she covers it up with yet another feeling, which is that she's being utterly self-indulgent to even think this way and she should stop being so damned self-centered and get on with her life.

But why does she feel strange, and then ungrateful, and then self-involved in the first place? And let's start at the beginning: Why does she feel she is not as good a wife as she should be? Why *isn't* she good enough just as she is?

She may say to herself, "So what if I'm not perfect? I'm doing as well as I can!" But why must she be perfect? Who says? If the Witness's voice is not her own conscience, if it is not her mother's, her father's, her husband's voice, whose voice is it? Who is this wife to whom it keeps comparing her? Her mother? Her grandmother? *Who?*

And how did this woman get so good?

3

The Wife

Re-vision—the act of looking back, of seeing with fresh
eyes, of entering an old text from a new critical
direction—is for us more than a chapter in cultural
history: it is an act of survival. Until we understand the
assumptions in which we are drenched we cannot know
ourselves.

—ADRIENNE RICH
"When We Dead Awaken: Writing as Re-vision"

THE LATE NOVELIST John Gardner once said that all stories
begin with an arrival or a departure. Ishmael arrives in New Bed-
ford; Anna gets off a train; Cathy dies; Darcy appears at the
party; someone comes or someone goes and the story begins.
The story of marriage begins with the arrival of the Wife, that
character we will call for the moment the heroine. The story the
Wife's arrival sets in motion, a story of happily-ever-after love
that historians call the marriage plot, is one propelled—as is any
good story—by the nature of its principal character.

There have always been wives; but the Wife has not always

been with us. Chaucer's wise and ribald Wife of Bath, or Shakespeare's witty, unruly Beatrice is not the Wife I'm talking about. Where and when did she enter, this almost superhuman paragon of goodness—and why? Reading and researching the story backward, trying to find answers, I stumbled on the moment of her arrival.

In the great halls of the Yale library, I came upon a genre of books called "conduct" books, which first appeared in the late seventeenth century and continued to be popular well into the nineteenth. With titles like *The Lady's New Year's Gift* (1688), *Maxims for Married Ladies* (1796), *A Father's Legacy to His Daughters* (1822), and *The Young Lady's Friend* (1847), they suggest intimate advice, entrusted lovingly. The earliest ones read, though, like housekeeping primers, offering exhaustive instructions on carving turkeys and cleaning chimneys. Later on, something else crept in, and the books became less about a wife's actual chores than about subtler burdens. The voices instructing her, their tones ranging from stern to wheedling to rhapsodic, sounded oddly familiar.

"The moment a woman enters into the nuptial state, she should look upon herself as a new being," announces one author, writing in the form of a letter addressed simply to a "niece." She should view herself as in "a new kind of existence," one that "requires more care, more temper, more conduct and solidity, than young women usually pretend to." She should look on the "trifles" that once "delighted her" as mere "baubles" of her past, for "the pleasing levities and agreeable fooleries of a girl are particularly disgusting in a wife."

"Scrupulous decorum" required her to give up her "trifling" past by "relinquishing all female" and particularly "male acquaintances" so she could focus more intently on her duties and her character. Because once in this new, perfect state, she had extraordinary responsibility. "How interesting and important are the duties devolved on females as WIVES . . . the counsellor and friend of the husband; who makes it her daily study to lighten his cares, to soothe his sorrows, and to augment his joys; who like a guardian angel watches over his interests." A wife's nature, another dulcet voice chimes in, is "a spirit that can accommodate itself to the wishes and humours of those on whom it is dependent for happiness."

A wife's nature was the subject of these books. Here's one, called *The Young Wife, or Duties of Woman in the Marriage Relation,* that cuts to the chase: Its first chapter is "Submission," then, in order, come "Kindness," "Cheerfulness," "Sympathy," "Delicacy and Modesty," "Love of Home," "Simplicity," "Neatness," "Punctuality," "Early Rising," "Domestic Economy," "Sobriety." On and on they go, leading the reader into a virtual nunnery called Marriage—indeed, I wondered why there seem to be no men in this or any other conduct book.

A wife learned not only how she was supposed to behave but who she was supposed to *be* in this new circumstance. She should be—again a nun comes to mind—simple, modest, thrifty, vigilant, pious, industrious, humble, and cheerful. "Love" was most often mentioned in the guises of dutifulness, appreciation. As *The Young Lady's Friend* summed up, "Love in the heart of a wife should partake largely of the nature of *Gratitude.* She should fill her soul with gratitude to God and to the Man who has chosen *her* to be his helpmate for time and for Eternity."

Each author seemed more obsessively interested than the last in the minutest details of a wife's demeanor and behavior, her dress, her interests, how she spends her time, even what she thinks about. She shouldn't read much, they felt, particularly "sentimental stories and books of mere entertainment," as "this species of reading cultivates what is called the heart prematurely, lowers the tone of the mind, and induces indifference for those common pleasures and occupations which, however trivial in themselves, constitute by far the greatest portion of our daily happiness." Conduct books impressed on women the idea of a very narrow horizon—intellectual, emotional, physical—as best suited to their "true" natures. "The female character should possess the mild and retiring virtues rather than the bold and dazzling ones; great eminence in almost anything is sometimes injurious to a young lady; whose temper and disposition should appear to be pliant rather than robust; to be ready to take impressions rather than to be decidedly marked." This uniquely flexible "female character" that brought happiness to everyone was increasingly abstract and idealized: "If a woman be herself pure and noble-hearted, she will come into every circle as a person does into a heated room who carries with him the freshness of the woods." Her pleasing nature gave her not power, exactly, but something infinitely subtler: "A principal source of your importance is the very great and extensive influence which you in general have with our sex," wrote James Fordyce in 1794 in one of his first *Sermons to Young Women.* Other authors also assured her that this influence was "enormous," "immense," and "vast," but only if, as scholar Judith Lowder Newton points out, it remained "secret," "unobserved"—an "undercurrent below the surface."

"The happiness of your life depends now on continuing to please a single person," Thomas Jefferson informed his newly married daughter, Martha, in 1790, and "to this all other objects must be secondary." Cadwallader Colden told his daughter Elizabeth likewise: "Let your Dress and your Conversation & the whole Business of your life be to please your Husband."

Another father told his newly married daughter that a man's pleasure would now depend entirely on her "good sense and good taste." Less optimistic about a young woman's ability to please her husband, another hoped "with the goodness of your disposition, and by following the counsel of wise friends, you might, in time, make yourself worthy" of the man she married. He promised to be her "director"—but only so long as she deserved it—"by letting you know how you are to act, and what you are to avoid." Other conduct books found it equally necessary to oversee her and divert her "from falling into the many errors, fopperies and follies to which [her] sex is subject."

Why did women suddenly need to be told how to be married—or rather, how to *be*?

I learned that conduct books had existed in England long before 1700, but for *men,* not women; they had been primers for teaching merchants and gentlemen aristocratic behavior. These books I was reading, though, were something new. They were for British and American *women* only, and the instruction they offered about marriage led women not into an aristocratic world of fox hunts and ballrooms, but inside the kitchen and drawing room.

The authors—pastors and doctors, moralists and women with prim, imposing, and contrived names such as the Countess Dowager of Carlisle, Miss Catherine E. Beecher, "the Rev. E. J. Hardy, A Graduate In The University Of Matrimony"—delivered their message in stilted, exacting prose and a preachy, schoolmarmish tone at once condescending and exhortative. When not painfully prudish, the authors were dreamily, gaudily poetic, drawing heavily on heavenly images—angels, usually— whenever they spoke of the wife. And when they spoke of their duties, they often cited poets, unnamed "friends" of women, the Bible, nature, and God, sometimes all at once, to make their most important points. "That *home* is her appropriate and appointed sphere of action there cannot be a shadow of doubt; for the dictates of nature are plain and imperative on this subject, and the injunctions given in Scripture no less explicit."

A Miss More points out, after a long introduction filled with agonizing, self-righteous humility—like some unctuous Dickensian character insinuating herself into the will—that women are like porcelain, and that we must "put the finest vases, and the costliest images in places of the greatest security, and most remote from any probability of accident or destruction," because "by being so situated, they find their protection in their weakness, and their safety in their delicacy." Miss More, along with the others, reassures a wife of her worth by adding that "this [porcelain vase on the shelf] metaphor is far from being used with a design of placing young ladies in a trivial, unimportant light; it is only introduced to insinuate, that where there is more beauty, and more weakness, there should be greater circumspection and superior prudence."

As I read on, I saw a wife's home becoming more than just a hearth to clean, but also a spiritual place of the heart. "There is an influence, there is an empire which belongs to you . . . I mean that which has the heart as its object," rhapsodized James Fordyce in 1794 in another of his Sermons to Young Women. "To man belongs the kingdom of the head, to woman the empire of the heart!" exulted James McGrigor Allan in *Woman Suffrage Wrong* (1890).

Home, like Wife, was earning a sentimental, obsessional attention. A woman of such inexhaustible goodness and boundless, uniquely female unconditional love—what one minister called "a pure, disinterested love, such as is seldom found in the busy walks of a selfish and calculating world"—dwelled not in a mere home, but in a nurturant, merciful heaven, a blissful realm where, as historian Nancy Cott observes, "the beatific rituals and emotions supposed to take place . . . attracted an almost fetishistic concern."

Her heart and her goodness were crucial in a world where a man's "feelings are frequently lacerated to the utmost point of endurance, by collisions, irritations, and disappointments. And to recover his equanimity and composure, home must be a place of repose, of peace, of cheerfulness, of comfort."

But.

A woman could displease a husband with the merest slip in her conduct, the smallest nick in her porcelain perfection. Besides having "apparent strength of character, which is liable to alarm both her own and the other sex; and to create admiration rather than affection," she could fall from grace by exhibiting any number of equally startling traits—envy, jealousy, scolding, talking, reading, thinking, even *knowing*. "As the first of all evils, as the source of calamity, as the source of all pain, avoid, O daughter of Eve, the bewitching charm of *curiosity*," Erasmus Darwin, one of the most esteemed and popular Victorian writers, urged, adding that she must be contented "with knowledge fitting for thee"—knowledge of the home.

Inquisitiveness was suspect: While conduct books urged

women to immerse themselves in the "agreeable" contempla-
tion of men's needs and desires, William Kenrick's *The Whole
Duty of Woman* warned, "Study not the ways of man," for they "are
dangerous and hard to find out." It seemed that, like Psyche,
promised the love of her new husband, Eros, only if she
promised never to look at or question him, a woman could earn
her husband's love only if she didn't see him, look at or ask
about his life, or know what he knew.

She could really displease him by spending money on
herself—particularly, one conduct book says, on "that violent
passion for *fine clothes,* so predominant in your sex" (emphasis
his). "Be not luxurious and extravagant. . . . affect not beyond
thy sphere," says another. Men would prefer "*cleanliness* and
sweetness of their person" over a "silly woman of quality." And
yet, she must not "attempt to destroy *his* innocent pleasures by
pretexts of economy; retrench rather your own expenses to pro-
mote them" (emphasis mine).

Clearly, these voices were not recommending an aristocratic lifestyle, which would have required fabulous self-display,
lavish expenditure, and knowledgeable, skillful speech and
conversation—all of which were actually expected of noblewomen as evidence of their lineage and education. Nor were
they addressing sturdy American Colonial wives, who were historically skilled and productive; they had been sextons, shoe-
makers, silversmiths, and doctors, just as their husbands were,
and while they had worked out of their homes, they did so
alongside their husbands, churning out food and clothes together, raising children together. No, this was something new.
Suddenly, here was a world of simple, modest efficiency experts,
and the persistent message was that their purpose was to focus

on "the real and deeply interesting effects which the conduct of their sex will always have on the happiness of society."

I couldn't help but wonder why wives' conduct, and not husbands', was all at once such an issue, why there was such an urgency to teach women some *other* kind of life, some other constellation of duties from ones they were familiar with, and some other person to be. Women were getting the message, though, learning to link, as they were supposed to, their conduct with their natures. And they were making other crucial connections urged on them by the books, like coupling their husbands' happiness with their behavior. And their *own* happiness with their behavior. "I know that the continuance of the first of my blessings—my husband's affection—depends in a degree on my own conduct," one young American wife wrote her sister in 1792, noting that "if I lose my hold on his affections I lose all I now have to make my life happy."

I read on. It seemed to be open season now, as more renowned, "literary" authors—Daniel Defoe, Jonathan Swift, Samuel Richardson, Jeremy Collier, Richard Steele, even feminist Mary Wollstonecraft!—put their collective hand in to paint a fuller picture of this frugal homebody who was, before my eyes, being perfected into a moral standard. Her original thrift and vigilance, her humility, modesty, and cleanliness were all still there, but these authors were—frantically, it seemed to me—developing something else in her, a psychologically "feminine" character that could be summed up in one word: *good*.

It is clear, reading old conduct books and advice literature today, that its authors were in search of someone who did not exist; that they were desperately creating something, not observing it. The Wife was simply being devised—or, rather, divined. It's impossible to imagine what real person these authors are invoking, since her virtuousness and radiance, her utter lack of vanity, aggression, and desire—all those characterological absences that, taken together, constituted a Wife's appeal and her influence—do not illustrate a recognizable woman. Instead what begins to come through is a shadowy ideal, a sort of collective hallucination, part child, part angel, part domestic servant. It's as if an entire culture got together to fantasize about God's own helpmate, personified it and called it a Wife. And then neglected to tell anyone why.

The greatest pains were being taken to prove how *unlike a man* this woman was, how unhappy in a man's world, how disinterested in "male" pursuits like making money and achieving, how uniquely, innately domestic and *female* her goodness was! What made a woman good was very different from what made a man good, and great pains were taken to divide character as well as the world by sex. "To man belong professions, dignities, authorities and pleasures; for woman, there remain only duties, domestic virtue, and perhaps as the result of these, the happiness of tranquil submission." That about said it. But while men's characters were left pretty much alone, the Wife's kept being obsessively improved; her unique, feminine goodness and propriety had to be ever more exhaustively purified, polished, and tamed.

By the late nineteenth century the Wife had been imbued with total moral perfection, and she had astounding moral responsibility in a marriage. She alone had the task of taming both man and society; of "transforming, even feminizing, an entire culture." Her goodness was unparalleled and unquestioned. "If anyone, male or female, dared to tamper with the complex of

Virtues which made up True Womanhood," historian Barbara Welter says, "he was damned immediately as an enemy of God, of Civilization, and of the Republic." That thousands upon thousands of pages were necessary to elaborate for the Wife the subtleties and nuances of her innate distinction not only from the male, but from all other kinds of women, did not provoke the reading public to question just how "innate" these distinctions could really be.

Why was it so urgent to convince women that "you have deep responsibilities; you have urgent claims; a nation's moral worth is in your keeping"? Something else was going on, something that women weren't being told directly; some truth was being obscured in the mounting, anxious adulation. In his book *Sesame and Lilies* (1865), John Ruskin's panic and over-the-top exaltation of the Wife finally did me in.

> But do you not see that . . . she must—as far as one can use such terms of a human creature—be incapable of error? So far as she rules, all must be right, or nothing is. She must be enduringly, incorruptibly good; instinctively, infallibly wise— wise not for self-development, but for self-renunciation: wise, not that she may set herself above her husband, but that she may never fail from his side: wise, not with the narrowness of insolent and loveless pride, but with the passionate gentleness of an infinitely variable, because infinitely applicable, modesty of service—the true changefulness of woman.

The complex cultural fantasy he was concocting drew me deeper into my questioning. This whole discussion of "true" women was so antiquated and bizarre—and yet so stunningly pertinent to the mood and behavior changes I was observing in the women I was speaking to! Newly married women today seemed to be responding to the very same injunctions about earning a husband's love and approval through their pleasing conduct. They felt, now, the same link between this conduct and maintaining a marriage; the same knotty involvement of this conduct with their own *happiness,* all elaborated so exhaustively in these three-hundred-year-old books. When Tracy stopped dancing because she felt it was somehow unseemly; when Antonia felt she'd be too "overwhelming" if she spoke openly about her sexual desires, their strange compulsion to adhere to *another standard of behavior* was what surprised me. Yet it was one clearly defined and delineated, *ad absurdum,* right here in these books and pamphlets and letters.

Why, I wondered, had women in England and in America snapped them up? Why had the genre mushroomed so wildly between the eighteenth and nineteenth centuries, with its rigidly gendered instructions on how to behave, who to *be,* in marriage? I desultorily picked up Webster's and the *Oxford English Dictionary* to look up the word *wife.* Maybe there I would find some definition, some clue to the identity of this woman who was being invented before my eyes in conduct books—and why. I looked randomly at various editions from the mid-1800s to the present. They were mostly similar, nothing unusual: "the lawful consort of a man" in 1856; "a married woman" in 1936. Sometimes they referred to the way *wife* is joined with other words—like *fishwife* or *alewife,* or, in Shakespeare's day, *strawberry wife*—to turn *wife* into "a woman of low employment." But in one recent edition of the *OED* (1986), there was a line added that I hadn't seen before: At one time, the word *wife* was "restricted to a woman of *humble rank* or low employment."

With the help of historians, I began to understand that the conduct books had a far greater task than merely to teach women how to care for their homes all by themselves, or even to convince them that they were naturally suited to domesticity and submission. They literally had to teach wives *who they were* in a culture being sharply split in two—into work and home, public and private, male and female.

Before conduct books, there was no such thing as "middle-class" life, or a "middle-class" wife, those bedrocks of our understanding of marriage—for there was as yet no middle class. In the England of 1700, there were the nobility and workers for the nobility; in America, there were laborers, artisans, farmers. The rules they lived by said that it was the social class you were born into that completely ruled and determined your life. If you were a poor girl born into a family that worked a piece of land, it was absurd to imagine living in a castle. There was no upward mobility through making money: You inherited your lot in life. Who your parents were, what class they were, how much money they had—that's who you were and that's what you had.

And that determined your hopes for marriage. What was "good" in a woman—that is, distinguished and desirable—was precisely the same as what was "good" in a man: fortune and class. And both were inherited. What made someone a "good," worthy, and useful marriage partner, then, were breeding and property. At the top, the good wife, like the good husband, was quite simply an aristocrat. Lower down the social hierarchy, she, like he, was a good laborer, or good for raising children. "Good" was not abstract. It was about survival. And it had nothing to do with gender.

At the time conduct books for women began to be written, all was changing. "Work" became defined more and more as what was done away from home. Now a man could make money in the harsh world of nascent capitalism, and a young man who worked a scrap of land *could* imagine owning the manor. There were suddenly more marriageable men with means who were not noblemen—but nowhere near enough noblewomen for them to marry.

Unmarried men of means—suddenly the terms were economic!—in search of brides would now have to look beyond family and fortune to other criteria of goodness.

But what criteria? What could be as tempting as a noble heritage had been? What could a woman of modest or no means and from an undistinguished family *have* that a prominent man with good earning potential might want? Whereas previously the desirable and often unattainable ideal was defined by sumptuous clothes, furniture, gardens, and other indicators of wealth and status, now a discerning, ambitious man had to have some way to recognize this new person who wore, as a horrified wedding guest in Jane Austen's *Emma* summed up, "a shocking lack of satin." Who *was* she?

That's where we came in.

It became a cultural necessity to weave satin out of muslin, to make men think they were getting something "good" in a woman who, just moments before, might not even have been marriageable at all. So, in order to describe—or, rather, create—a whole new kind of enticing value in a woman, and to educate both sexes about what that "value" was, conduct books were born. And in them (and later, in novels) arose a fantastic creature whose currency was no longer wealth and class. Now what was "good" in a wife would simply have to be what men going off to work needed most: domestic usefulness and a modest, self-renouncing character to advertise and adorn it.

The birth of the middle-class Wife is also the birth of a woman's consciousness of the self—of *her* self—as a moral project. With proper vigilance and constant monitoring she could now transform herself into someone "good" and worthy and moral enough to win a husband and earn his love. This notion of women's self-perfectibility was as new as the notion of *making* money, rather than inheriting it, was for men. A man was learning for the first time to pursue a goal, while, simultaneously, a woman learned to *become* the goal.

Although goodness in women (particularly chastity and sexual fidelity) has worried every culture since long before biblical times, never before was the word *wife* so equated with the word *virtue* and that virtue itemized so painstakingly and precisely. It was the conduct books' purpose, at first, not only to conjure up and then anatomize this ideal woman, but to convince real women that staying home was the *best* job—and simultaneously, to divert them from the fact that it was now their *only* job. The coaching tone and rhapsodic images of a domestic heaven over which a cheerful angel would preside hid a painful agenda: to make it clear to women that the era of partnership was over. The world where married couples had worked side by side, sharing the pains and pleasures of economic, social, and political life, had ended.

But the writers of conduct books never said as much. They never admitted that women were no longer welcome in the work world, or in the social or political worlds—an omission that may or may not have been conscious. They never addressed politics or economics at all; it was as if all that didn't exist. Instead, the books detached and polarized the world into public and private, economic and domestic—men and women. They split the human psyche, too, turning men and women into emotional, psychological, characterological opposites, and a "female" psychology was thus born. While prior to 1800 men and women were not regarded as identical, "in that epoch ideas about the qualities that men and women *shared* had been balanced against the perceived differences," Sheila Rothman notes (emphasis hers). Now that they no longer shared the same world, "the attributes shared by both sexes were more or less forgotten. Qualities of mind and character were seen as applying to one sex or the other—almost never to both." Now men and women were seen as being severed from each other by nature and by personality rather than by circumstance. Men were exiled to one planet, women imprisoned on another, and we forgot that both once lived together on earth.

Conduct books relentlessly refined the Wife's humble, self-sacrificing "virtues" until everyone not only knew who she was but knew the precise tilt of her head, the warm expression on her cheerful face, the angelic expanse of her brow, the arc of her loving arms. While the economic structure of society was being remade from the ground up, while money was replacing birthright and factories were replacing land as the basis of wealth, culture staged a diversion. The entrancing, riveting play became all about what was and wasn't *good*. An amazing thing had happened: Women's bodies and character became the stage on which the changing scenery of society pivoted, and a morality tale was acted out.

In less than a century, a chaste home economist and eagle-eyed efficiency expert had been constructed, manufactured, and merchandised as the one standard for all classes of a perfect Wife. In reality, this Wife was needed to fill that economic and cultural hole that had not yet been dubbed the middle class. So she had to be sold, and the job of the conduct books was to portray her irresistibly as the only woman worth having and being. To do so, they seized on a clever trope: an inversion of previous values. The modest Wife outshone her richer, shinier aristocratic predecessor with her luminous inner glow rather than her glittering outward gloss. Her extraordinary inherent *femaleness* simply trumped her moneyed, elegant predecessor, who was now declared all surface and silliness, extravagance and idleness.

If the aristocracy and all it stood for was now equated with spiritual and moral corruption—the greedy Bingley sisters instead of the glowing Bennet girls—the new all-male, economic sphere, which might have its rough-and-tumble attractions, was deliberately equated with cruelty and emotional emptiness. The Wife, through conduct books' careful calculation, became what scholar Nancy Armstrong calls a "creature of feelings" symbolic of an angelic goodness and unselfishness unavailable in anyone but her. She alone could magically transform men from the hassled, distracted workers they had become into happy, peaceful, responsive husbands. In one bold stroke, this image of the Wife had captured the imaginations of desirable men and aspiring women. This unreal creature who had no ambitions outside her designated sphere desired nothing more, conveniently, than to marry, then manage her husband's home with the newly prized vigilance, thrift, grace, imagination, taste, discretion, and heart. And so a bargain was struck: In exchange for dominance over the domestic sphere, a woman gave up her identity and even any desires pertaining to the outside world—for money, achievement, or power of her own.

But the deal she was offered was one she literally could not refuse if she wanted a home, a living wage, and a life in the new order. Because her acceptance of her role was essential to bringing in capitalism, lurking under the conduct books' seductive language was a thinly disguised and very literal threat: in the words of Ann Douglas in *The Feminization of American Culture* (1977), "Stay within your proper confines and you will be worshiped, step outside and you will cease to exist."

WHAT MUST THIS transition into middle-class life have felt like? For men it must have been terrifying but simultaneously thrilling, because of the extraordinary new possibilities and opportunities that in the prior order had simply not existed. But the loss of daily connection with their families must have been wrenching, and the mounting idealization of home as a "spiritual sanctuary," an "oasis in the desert," a "safe haven in a heartless world," speaks to and attempts to compensate for this loss, as did the Wife as "angel in the house." One can see, though, from a man's point of view, the anxious need for model behavior in this Wife, who was, after all, left home alone all day. One can appreciate, too, the value to him of her huge, loving, nurturant, virtuous heart, which, while it would have no place in the callous world of work, would be waiting to welcome him home. And yet, whether a husband registered it consciously, he had lost a more prosaic lover, the daily involvement with a real-life, thriving partner. And no ideal, no angel, no matter how perfect and perfectly loving, could make up for that.

For women, it was terrifying—but hardly thrilling. The extraordinary forces that had brought a cataclysmic change that gave men hope, opportunity, and movement in society had left women stranded, with neither social nor economic worth. Rather than having the protection of being born into a social class and a way of living, as they once had, where they shared with men work and sex and the drama of life, now women truly had no place. They were on their own, hurled into a sexually dangerous world where they had no way of making a living that wasn't potentially life-threatening.

A woman could be a spinster, a prostitute, a factory drudge—or a Wife. Being a Wife, though, now meant something different from being a wife. Now it meant, for the first time, an exchange of protection and a place off the streets for exclusive sexual access and domestic perfection. You had no choice but to aspire to the ideal of being a full-time guardian of the home and its inhabitants—and a cheerful guardian, at that. (There really was no other option, sociologist Arlene Skolnick says, citing evidence that over the course of the nineteenth century even "lower-class families preferred to send children, rather than wives, out to work to supplement the family income," so that by 1890 "only about two percent of married women were employed outside the home.") So what do you do?

Conduct books told you: Make yourself indispensible to this new man.

As fortunate as women must have felt to have *any* sphere of their own in this new economy that had excised them from economically valued work in it—and the vast success of conduct books attest to women's need—they must also have mourned the disorienting loss of connection and paid productivity, of a place in the world, of a home that was once a home to power, where men and women were neither idealized nor polarized. With the economic, political, and social worlds now closed to them, though, and no dowries or income through which to experience some measure of freedom and control, all they could hope for, given men's need for sanctuary and their own for security and safety, was home and virtue.

In response to men's idealization of what they had lost; in response to women's terror of losing their lives, women agreed to be that angel—to accept the bizarre new polarizations, to give up their lustiness, their income, their curiosity, their opinions, their knowledge. Women became physically, financially, and emotionally dependent on keeping a man happy, in order to have a place in the world—that "safety," "security," and "protection" to shelve that priceless porcelain that the conduct books keep harping on. They tried to embody men's longings as their part in this bargain, accepting responsibility for satisfying men's desires as the road to survival and identity—and love. They tried, too, to put aside desire, assertion, anger, and frustration and adopt a new, perfect self.

What did it mean to have to undergo such contortions, to cover up such gaping wounds, to be privy to or excluded from entire categories of personality and knowledge, newly dubbed "male" and "female"? What did it feel like to have your acknowledged participation and productivity vanish along with your sexuality? You might forget that loss, as you become invested in its replacement and dependent on all the benefits of the new order. You might begin to defend and justify the replacement as years go by and you lose the sense of what it was you lost. But you would be constantly reminded, if you so much as glanced outside your sphere, or used the word *control* rather than *oversee,* or *power* rather than *influence,* or had a sexual, rather than a pious thought, that you were, as Arlene Skolnick observes, "held hostage to values that men both cherished and violated in their daily lives."

What kind of love could there be in such a pairing of isolated icons—between explicitly virtuous domestic woman and implicitly amoral economic man? How does one even speak of love when one of the lovers has been disembodied, left with no voice, no sexuality? In 1896, Sigmund Freud spoke of the resulting hysteria when he observed the lively, sexual women who came to psychoanalysis for what one patient called the "talking cure." He tried hypnosis, free association, anything he could think of, to free them from bizarre symptoms that he found to be most frequently resulting from "a loss of voice."

Husbands and wives were offered a stereotype for a partner, instead of the real one they had once shared their lives with. They were given rationalizations for their new estrangement and their sudden, supposedly inherent limitations—the different psychologies, natures, biologies, languages, characters that decreed and justified this brutal rupture. Nothing, though, not the birth of female psychology nor the notion of a "true" "feminine" nature, nor even the insistence on a "natural" female moral conduct, could assuage the pain and nostalgia I imagine married men and women must have felt at their separation from each other, the hasty barriers erected to each other's worlds, words, natures, bodies, knowledge, and morals. It's no surprise that sociologists call the nineteenth century, as historian John Demos does, "a time of troubles, not to say tragedy, in the history of the family."

The new, middle-class version of love and marriage was quite a story. Not only its plotline and its heroine had been domesticated, but also its dialogue.

As a flesh-and-blood woman was supposed to become a self-sacrificing, virtuous Wife, a whole, rich vocabulary had to be revised, given entirely new meanings—just as *wife* was, and *good* was—in order to shape and reflect this new morality suddenly focused so intently on women's conduct. In making *female* the characterological and psychological opposite of *male,* and *wife* the moral, "better half" of *husband,* a battalion of familiar words and concepts had to be divvied up by gender and polarized just as men and women had been. Words themselves were emptied of their real meanings, and new, more appropriately "feminine" and "masculine" meanings installed.

Lady, once a term defining a woman of the upper class or, in America, from a wealthy family, now was defined as a woman who "observed the properties of the woman's sphere." By this definition, you could *become* a lady, even if you weren't born one, by staying at home and behaving in what was considered a "proper" way: devoting yourself to your husband and children! *Lady* thus became just another word for Wife, synonyms for attainable status symbols elevated, as Gerda Lerner points out in *The Lady and the Mill Girl,* to "the accepted ideal of femininity toward which all women would strive."

The word *proper,* which had once referred to the aristocratic male's behavior, dress, and manners, also became a word applying to women's behavior alone. So did the word *noble,* which had once meant "titled" (or, in eighteenth-century America, "wealthy") but now meant "domestic," "humble," "virtuous," and "self-sacrificing," yet another description of the Wife.

Whereas *noble* and *proper* became "feminine" words, reserved exclusively for the Wife, *power* and *work* went over to men, thereby being spared any moral tinge. (Women's *influence,* on the other hand, unlike power so silent, secretive, and careful, was ablaze with moral overtones.) *Work* no longer applied to work done in the home and, therefore, work done by a woman, but only to labor in the public sphere, done by men. And conduct books stifled women inclined even to conceive of the word *work* to describe what they did, as homemaking took on the exhilarating aura of an art form, a God-given and extraordinarily creative mission perfectly suited to the uniquely spiritual, even mystical talents of the Wife. Critical of any wife who did not envision her duties through this spiritual, moral, magical lens, conduct books finally censured any reader who considered herself to be in a "role" doing "work" at all.

In order to be a "lady," "noble" and "proper," then, a wife's goodness required her, among other things, to *not know* she was doing work, to *not say* or *feel* that it was work, and to *not be unhappy* that the not-work she was doing was unpaid not-work.

Look what happened to sex: *Desire, sexual,* and *pleasure* were now male words exclusively, an astonishing feat, since women, after all, had long been considered especially sensual and even more lusty than men. But now, pressured to adopt a "proper" sexual nature—that is, no desire at all—they wound up with the newly exalted "feminine" condition historian Nancy Cott has called "passionlessness," the height of the Wife's morality. For *desire* now meant being desired, and *pleasure* meant being pleasing. A good woman could only be the object, not the subject, of any verb meaning "to want."

By the late 1800s, it would be said that it was Darwinian evo-

lution that had done away with ladies' sexual desire, leaving
them, as one historian puts it, no more than "overbred evolutionary anachronisms" whose uteruses had become diseased
from their excessively high development. Only "low" women,
the story went, as opposed to distinguished middle-class women,
"suffered from the indignity of sexual desire."

This odd arrangement between desirous men and desireless
women became the idealized moral relationship between the
new middle-class economic husband and his domestic Wife.
Women were left with no respectable alternative, and men left
only with "respectable" wives.

"Give up your sexuality, that is, your pleasure, your embodied
self, and you will be safe, protected, respected, and secure": This
was the real deal a woman was offered, and she felt the necessity
in her gut. "And if you don't, you may even lose your life." Im-
plicit in the conduct books' fulsome praise of the Wife was a
scathing indictment of any woman who fell short of the ideal,
whose desires hadn't yet been regulated, controlled, shaped,
and, finally, excised from her body. Any woman who had not yet
subverted the needy, lusty, creative, instinctive self she was born
with and installed in their place, eager servitude, sexlessness,
passivity, and self-sacrifice was "licentious," a witch, perhaps, a
madwoman with a diseased uterus. The Wife was offered everything society called desirable in exchange for voicing no further
desires—that is, in exchange for her voice. And her sexuality.
And a capacity for policing herself to maintain the highest
moral standards—the internalized voice of the Witness.

As her desires became fewer and fewer, and she acquired
greater and greater stature and worth to men, children, and society, her very substance vaporized. She had no more to give.

She became airier, hollower by the decade, until the Victorian Wife's total vacancy was heralded as sacred. Praise for her silence, her self-restraint, her self-abnegation, her selflessness—a catalog of curtailment, a bevy of suffixes restraining, containing, and diminishing, disembodying, and denying the word *self*—reached an ecstatic fusion as authors wrote her into a characterological corner. The qualities most adored in her were, finally, absences, negatives.

This Wife, the "true" woman with so much influence to "soften hearts and polish manners," "to redeem as well as to please men," had a strange problem: *There was nothing inside her.* She was empty, weightless, wantless.

THE WIFE WAS an astonishing construct and had awesome power; her creation turned the aristocratic household in England and the Colonial household in America—both governed by a man—into middle-class households overseen by a woman. Yet her rise meant the downfall of real women's authority and authenticity; it meant that conducting themselves the way she would—exclusively for the well-being of others—was the only sure way to a man's heart. The moral conduct of an icon was the conduct by which a wife would be hereafter judged.

It is the Wife's staggering impact on the formation of middle-class life that accounts for her haunting presence in our lives today, three hundred years later. She alone remains a template, the shadowy heroine of the marriage plot, the mysterious, morally exalted creature who is presented by the Witness to every bride. The words once used to describe the particulars of her character, and the deal she was offered by the culture, are as ancient and forgotten now as a Greek chorus, but they still resonate. And the Witness, that nagging voice of the conduct books, is there to remind a woman, always, of the good deal she is being offered and of the hazards she faces if she falls short of being good.

No wonder modern women have trouble with terms like *pleasure* and *desire, femininity* and *sexuality.* No wonder magazines—modern conduct books—still grapple with those words' extraordinary capacity, still, to wound us or endorse us (FEMININITY: WHAT ARE THE RULES NOW? asked the top coverline on *Elle* magazine in May 1996; and then, under it, as if to ridicule the quaintness of the very idea of rules, AND DO YOU CARE?). No wonder romance novels—disguised, sugar-coated conduct books—still promise even the plainest women the triumph of a fabulously rich and sexy man if she's trustworthy, nurturing, and virtuous. No wonder experienced modern wives, for whom the very notion of passionlessness is ridiculous, still succumb to rules of husband-catching and -keeping, as if spellbound, and as if marriage—not the man, not love, not even her own feelings—were all that mattered.

The dusty words and ruthless tone of the conduct books still echo in a new bride's ear, dictating the revision of behavior and feelings that we have seen, urging her toward a symbol, a stereotype, bringing with it as its shadow a darkening of mood. In obedience to that revision, Judy doesn't speak to her sister about how she feels now that she's married, because it differs so from the gratitude and cheerfulness she is supposed to feel. She knows that *marriage in itself should make women happy.* Tracy, overseeing her husband's food and alcohol intake, is trying to fit herself into a role that requires her to *think of the well-being of her husband first* and dance later. Antonia understands that however wild she was before, *a good wife is not sexual.* Kyra is obsessed with safety, protection, and security—her own and everyone else's—because she knows that *a wife's happiness depends on marriage, and marriage, in turn, requires constant vigilance.* Tami no longer jots fiery hopes and passions into her journal, Sarah downplays the importance of her past adventures, and Greta reduces the number of sexual partners she's had, because they all know that *single life is slightly shabby next to the more elevated condition of being a wife.*

"The way to gain love in marriage is to give up yourself." Today that sounds nonsensical, but it's a statement we are still compelled by, to our embarrassment and confusion. Our psyches and emotions, and therefore our expectations, have not caught up with our new economic and cultural circumstances, which are, after all, only decades old.

SO I FOUND my heroine. She had been drafted into a carefully plotted script, elevated so far above living women that they had no choice—if they wanted marriage—but to imitate her. The story the Wife's arrival might have set in motion instead came to a halt, leaving us with a romantic plot that lacks suspense, humor, warmth, sex, the fluidity and ambiguity and dissonance and motion of real life; it is instead static, rigid, perfect, inhabited not by a person but by a thing, an inhuman creature that cannot propel *any* story forward because it has no character to develop. The heroine is a monster—which *Webster's* says can also mean a "person of unnatural excellence, as a *monster* of inhumanity, or of perfection."

So now we know how the story goes—or rather, doesn't go—inside that perfect little white cottage of domestic bliss, with its perfect Wife. But let's not stomp out and slam the door just yet. Before we devise a plot that can really thicken, let's take a good look around, for real wives are still trying to live there—we ourselves may still be. Now, though, we can turn on all the lights and throw open the windows and doors.

4

The Ghost of Marriage Past

No more alone sleeping, no more alone waking
   thy dreams divided, thy prayers in twain;
Thy merry sisters tonight forsaking,
   Never shall we see, maiden, again.

Never shall we see thee, thine eyes glancing,
   Flashing with laughter and wild in glee,
Under the mistletoe kissing and dancing,
   Wantonly free.

There shall come a matron walking sedately,
   Low-voiced, gentle, wise in reply.
Tell me, O tell me, can I love her greatly?
   All for her sake must the maiden die?

      —MARY COLERIDGE
      "Marriage"

DURING THE RESEARCH for my last book, I first began to notice that women often adopt, or feel they should adopt, the particular qualities we call "goodness" in the Wife. It struck me then that many of the women who could impersonate most vividly the

Wife's manner, her way of speaking and moving and gesturing, were too young to know who she was. They had not read about her in conduct books; they may or may not have had mothers or grandmothers who resembled her. They hadn't seen her on *The Donna Reed Show.* They did not know, or care, about "separate spheres." They were too young even to have known a world in which most women were housewives, one in which "goodness" meant that peculiar combination of cheerful submissiveness and quiet, steely dominance that characterized the female stars of those cloyingly chipper sitcoms of the fifties: *Father Knows Best, Ozzie and Harriet, Leave It to Beaver.*

How, if they'd never seen or heard her, could these young modern women mimic so brilliantly and precisely the sing-songy chirpiness, the frozen smile, the eager, accommodating gesture—an act so stunningly saccharine it made my teeth ache? I watched as woman after woman, as if sent by central casting to star in the role, recreated with breathless effusiveness the Wife's constellation of blandly "positive" attributes: her perky compliance, her apprehensive politeness, her mannered innocence. Here was fake sincerity communicated in horrifyingly perfect pitch. Here, I thought, was good-womanness personified, and all the women I met seemed to have her in their repertoire.

They obviously didn't have to have seen *The Donna Reed Show* to know her. They just *knew* her, picked up her image and her insidiousness somehow—but how?—in some other life, some other dimension—but where? It's as if women have inherited a trait, like musical talent or good hand-eye coordination, that compels us to recognize and reproduce her; some atavistic attribute, the psychological equivalent of a vestigial tail.

The women I have spoken with understand viscerally how obsolete this character is, how poisonous her goodness, and yet how alive in our collective unconscious, still comforting men and capturing the hearts of a world that insists she's long gone. And they both know how suited she is to winning love, earning approval, and yet wonder why such a sexless, phony creature could be idealized by men.

I saw, too, that this Wife they could recreate so brilliantly was more treacherous than just any character they could step into and out of at will; she also had the peculiar power to diminish them, as though just being in her shoes for a moment assured that their own shoes would hurt afterward. I wrote in my last book:

> Becoming Donna Reed quite often began for these women with an attempt to do whatever was necessary not to feel grotesque next to her. They rarely complained of feeling "too small" by comparison; rather, they felt . . . overwhelming. They understood implicitly that the Donna Reed model is thinner, quieter, nicer, purer, and more feminine than they were. Some felt immediately "too large" or "too fat"—others just began over time to feel "too bossy" or "too independent" or "too complicated." Or "too loud" or "too noisy" or "too emotional" or "too sexual." Next to Donna Reed, who mainly listens and occasionally advises wisely, they felt they were "too talkative," too.

But how and why has this been happening to middle-class women, generation after generation, for nearly three hundred years now? My friend Elizabeth Debold and I are discussing this question for the hundredth time. She is a psychologist and the author of *Mother-Daughter Revolution: From Good Girls to Great Women,* a book about how mothers and daughters can stay connected as daughters grow into young women. The uncanny thing, we have noticed, is that at each transition point in a woman's life—first becoming a woman, next becoming a wife, and then becoming a mother—she experiences this same internal pressure to be *perfect*. I remark that each is a different experience of sexuality—the first, becoming sexually mature; the second, becoming lawfully sexually active; and the third, becoming sexually procreative. Why, at these particular celebrated moments of a woman's life, when she's arrived, does she tend to vanish under the weight of an ideal, of a need to be perfect—that is, not sexual? How could it be that at moments of sexual fruition and triumph the vision of a lusty, powerful, loving, sexual self actually eludes her and is replaced by a passionless fake?

"I think the fact that there's a resonance with what happened to women nearly three centuries ago, when the Wife was born, is not an accident," Elizabeth says. "Just as marriageable women [in the last chapter] saw themselves without a place and in incredibly dangerous circumstances, so do adolescent girls, as their bodies change and they begin to be seen as sexual beings, and begin to experience the powerful currents of sexual desire, find themselves in a sexually dangerous world. When that happens, part of a girl's psyche splits off and becomes ever watchful so that she doesn't attract dangerous or unwanted sexual attention. The way middle-class girls learn to attract love, rather than disapproval or potential violation, is by being cheerful, compliant and not sexual."

Sound familiar?

Like eighteenth-century wives endlessly attempting to perfect

and desexualize themselves in order to have and hold the marriages that they want and need so desperately, girls are willing to
reimagine themselves, to aspire to a more pleasing and "good"
ideal of girlhood, in order to hold on to *their* precious relationships as they move into the world of dating and of boys. Moreover, every relationship in their lives is threatened. They
become the object of attention from boys; they become threatening to their girlfriends; and adult women in their lives, anxious to protect them, encourage their "goodness." And so they
become disconnected from themselves—from the power of
their own feelings—and from others, as the earlier version of
the Witness offers safety in exchange for compliant conduct.
Goodness becomes their anchor, too, when the seas of authenticity in which their relationships once floated contentedly now
threaten to drown them.

"Why does this Witness speak so powerfully to wives?" Elizabeth wonders. What fears, and what changes, are occurring that
would call forth this same impulse for vigilance and perfection?

From what I hear from women, once their entire universe of
independence and multiple relationships changes and suddenly becomes invested in this one person, their husband, they
feel terrified of losing it—even though they know they can survive, even thrive, outside of marriage. At this very moment, the
Witness begins to put pressure on them, suggesting that nothing
short of perfection will keep him—and that, if she loses him, she
will have lost everything. The moment there is this much fear,
this much confusion and pressure, this much need for safety
and love when everything around you is changing—as it is when
you marry—there it is again, that familiar symbol of feminine
goodness and silence and cheerfulness, the Wife. She will solve

the problem, she will make a new wife safe. She alone is perfectly able to make one man happy so a wife will never be left—and left alone.

Once this psychic split first occurs—creating this extraordinary vigilance, turning a girl or woman into a spectator of herself—it recurs, like an earthquake might along a fragile fault line, every time there's another similar danger, a threat of a rupture of relationship. The split-off presence comes back to life larger each time. And with each recurrence, a woman is split once again from her true feelings, sense of power, and sexuality. It takes so little: A husband need only cock an eyebrow, look askance, to elicit in his wife this ancient fear—and to call up for her the image of the perfect Wife.

WE DO NOT think of ourselves as being able to "inherit" an ideal the way we inherit, say, curly hair or a tendency to plumpness; science has taught us that only that which is genetic is passed down from generation to generation. But the study of language reveals a very different source of inheritance. Evolutionary biologist Richard Dawkins, in his classic book, *The Selfish Gene,* observes that language seems to evolve by nongenetic means, "and at a rate which is orders of magnitude faster than genetic evolution." Language, it seems, is passed along by mimicry.

If language were passed down genetically, Dawkins argues, modern relatives of Geoffrey Chaucer would easily comprehend Chaucerian English. Yet Chaucer "could not hold a comprehensive conversation with a modern Englishman, even though they are linked to each other by an unbroken [genetic] chain of some twenty generations of Englishmen." Similarly, the Valley-girl speech pattern, beginning every sentence with a "like" and ending it with a question mark, is one that would leave Nathaniel Hawthorne clueless.

Dawkins first observed examples of this nongenetic cultural transmission among birds called saddlebacks, who live on the islands off New Zealand. Young saddleback males seemed to pick up distinct song patterns not from their fathers but from their territorial neighbors, like teenagers who use their friends', not their parents', language.

But language turns out not to be the only trait that human beings pick up nongenetically. Other crucial attitudes and behaviors come to us by way of something other than genes. Dawkins was fascinated by "the immense differences between human cultures around the world, from the utter selfishness of the Ik of Uganda as described by Colin Turnbull to the gentle altruism of Margaret Mead's Arapesh," and concluded that something nongenetic, even nonmaterial, some heady ingredient ladled out from the stew of human culture, fueled our very natures, an essence so pungent and potent that it transformed the course of human development.

If we are to understand, say, the evolution of the modern woman, "we must begin by throwing out the gene as the sole basis of our ideas on evolution," Dawkins decided. We'd need the name for another replicator, the equivalent of a gene, but one that "conveys the idea of a unit of cultural transmission, or a unit of *imitation*" (emphasis his). Dawkins named his unit a "meme"—rhymes with *cream*—short for *mineme*, a unit of imitation, as in *mimicry*. He liked the word, so resonant of "memory" but so close in sound and brevity to *gene*.

Memes are to our minds what genes are to our bodies, ideas that have the power to determine the way we think in the same way genes have the power to determine, say, the way we look. Memes are inherited ways of thinking, habits, the cultural equivalent of genes: "Just as genes propagate themselves in the gene pool by leaping from body to body via sperms or eggs," Dawkins explains, "so memes propagate themselves in the meme pool by leaping from brain to brain via a process which, in the broad sense, can be called imitation." Once rap came along, for instance, our understanding of music changed, just as, once Valley-girl speech appeared, an entire generation not only began and ended sentences differently but adopted a uniquely 1990s timbre, rhythm, and vocabulary. Our notion of sports changed after the invention of bungee-jumping; book publishing changed after word processors and blockbusters; "chic" was altered forever once fashion editors worldwide began wearing all black.

All these fashions and fancies shoot across datelines and time zones by memes. Fads—like, say, platform shoes—are meme-driven, but so are big ideas, like Christianity or individualism. Our ceremonies and our customs, our art, engineering, architecture, and technology, how we make candles, how we dance, and what we sing all contribute to the way we are. We've got to be *taught* to hate and fear, the song says, and indeed racism too is passed along by memes, proving that these little transmitters can sometimes be as malevolent as viruses (Wilhelm Reich called prejudice an "emotional plague"). Scientist Howard Rheingold sees human consciousness itself as a medley of memes.

Once passed down, these ideas and ideals stay with us; they *do* infect our consciousness the way viruses infect our bodies, propagating, mutating, and becoming resistant to uprooting. They are, Dawkins feels, as important to the process of human evolution as genes are; that is, *culture itself* is as influential in the course of human evolution as genes.

A whole science has grown up around the little meme. "The meme," *New York Times* columnist Edward Rothstein wrote recently, "has evolved from a rough metaphor into the basis of a discipline known as 'memetics.' " It has infected the work of computer scientists, philosophers, and even other biologists, as memes have worked their way into the core of our thinking about philosophy, computer science, sociopolitical biology. A meme leaping from one brain to another is acting much the way a parasite does—in fact, Dawkins calls the meme an "informational parasite"—feeding, once it has landed in the soft, warm medium of our minds, on all else that we ingest: books, music, arguments, images, fads, fashions, ceremonies, religion, and art. A meme eats up the jazz we listen to, thrives on the weddings we attend, and gobbles up the politicians' speeches we hear. After a feeding frenzy of just such fare, the attached memes spread, replicate, mutate, cause mutations. And "they don't let go until replaced," Rothstein observes, "unless displaced by rival memes."

NOW YOU'RE BEGINNING to understand why the Wife means a lot in marriage. In fact, according to Dawkins, icons—ideas too great and concepts too grand in scale to be easily lost—are not only passed along but passed among contemporaries quite intact from generation to generation. The idea of God, for instance:

We do not know how it arose in the meme pool. Probably it originated many times by independent "mutation." In any case, it is very old indeed. How does it replicate itself? By the spoken and written word, aided by great music and great art. Why does it have such high survival value? Remember that "survival value" here does not mean value for a gene in a gene pool, but value for a meme in a meme pool. The question really means: What is it about the idea of a god which gives it its stability and penetrance in the cultural environment? The survival value of the god meme in the meme pool results from its great psychological appeal. It provides a superficially plausible answer to deep and troubling questions about existence. It suggests that injustices in this world may be rectified in the next. The "everlasting arms" hold out a cushion against our own inadequacies.

It is through memes, I began to suspect, that the Wife's symbolic goodness is so perfectly passed along to women who don't "know" her. I checked my suspicion with Dr. Dawkins, and he agrees. The Wife, after all, is an icon that seems to have much in common with religious ideas (think *saint*). It boasts a goodness that was crafted into it centuries ago; it has appeared with many different faces and styles, mutating slightly as it hopped from the brain of, say, the wan, frail Victorian wife to that of the hardy, fit, fast-track mom. But the Wife, as an icon, endures, its essence intact, *because of its extraordinary psychological value.*

Remember that the Wife was created and idealized during a time of total, fundamental societal change, when everything was fluctuating in what for ages had been an orderly culture prescribed by rank and fortune. Particularly during times like this, times of stress, fear, danger, threat, the symbolic becomes extraordinarily important as an anchor for safety. Once women became valued for goodness rather than genealogy, they held on so to the *symbol* of this highly valued Wife because their world was changing so rapidly they didn't know how they would live without her; when their place, their work, their whole world no longer existed and they were scared.

Because the Wife is an idea too great, on a scale too grand to be easily lost, because she represents safety still, her memes just keep propagating, varying, mutating, and will not let go. They live on decade after decade in our mental and emotional circuitry—women's and men's alike—insinuating themselves into our very understanding of marriage and forming our expectations of who we are to be, once wed. The Wife, in ever new forms, is still reproduced endlessly in our modern conduct books—magazines—and in novels, plays, and television shows, movies and songs, relentlessly reshaping our desires, our dreams, the course of our personal development, and our marriages.

The ever vigilant Witness, guardian of the institution of marriage, preserver of the Wife's virtues, proclaims the icon's importance and her place in marriage, much the way a religion proclaims and spreads the word about its particular icons. The Witness whispering in our ears assures women's eerie wisdom about the icon's every move, her function, her influential goodness. The Witness, who arrives right at or just before the most important ceremony in women's lives—remember, ceremonies are passed down just the way icons, fads, and fancies are—insures that we no longer can think of being married without thinking of the idea of Wife. The Wife has so infected our thinking that we cannot even imagine marriage without her. (Think of all those women who cared little about diamonds until they became engaged and then, suddenly, could think of nothing else *but;* or the woman we saw earlier who had the "urge" to cook the moment she had that rock on her finger.) Her memes have "infected" us, taken on life within us. We know her every move.

Scientist Rupert Sheldrake posits another nongenetic mechanism of inheritance, which he calls "morphic resonance." Using dinosaurs as an example, he speaks of nonphysical "morphogenetic fields" that encode and store the form of preexisting beings over millions of years—fields that persist and "remember" these beings long after they are gone. Sheldrake says that we "tune in" to the past and to our similar predecessors through resonance; that we can sense, *feel,* what our forebears were like and even how they behaved, and that this resonance guarantees our resemblance to them, shaping us to their form, impelling us to carry on much the way they did. Our ceremonies and our rituals—like weddings—are the timeless devices by which we "tune in" to our predecessors and recall and repeat their ways; they enable us to get onto the same wavelength with, say, the Wife. It is through these rituals that we invoke the still-potent past, perpetuate its key features in the present, and reestablish who we are now.

The Wife remains in us, gathering might and resonance, unchallenged by any other icon, constantly reinvigorated over the centuries by politicians and pastors, by moralists and magazines, gathering strength in our middle-class milieu in much the same way that the guru of a religious cult can gather strength within that group over time, ultimately becoming so powerful that followers who may not even know that leader personally will sacrifice themselves for the sake of his image.

The Wife, like that leader, may not be anyone we know. It may not be our mothers or our grandmothers who have shown us how to "do" the Wife, but the world has, through our stories and our customs, our white wedding dresses and our diamond rings and our nursery rhymes, and our traditional middle-class family values, which ascribe to wives the role of guarding home and relationships, caring for the sick, the needy, and the young, morally reforming men and society, a role first formulated almost three centuries ago.

The psychological appeal of the Wife is, I believe, on the secular plane, as compelling as the idea of a god, assuring her the same "high survival value" in the meme pool and "stability and penetrance in the cultural environment." The Wife has long provided something everyone wants: a person to create and take care of the world of the home and to love and nurture its inhabitants; someone whose very pleasure it is to please them. The idea of Wife suggests, as does the idea of a god, that, as Dawkins puts it, the cares of the world will be eased, or even erased, by a benevolent and caring heart; and that the home will be a place of comfort and nurturance while her arms "hold out a cushion" against everyone's inadequacies. This was the precise emotional and psychological niche the Wife was *created* to fit when she was imagined so long ago; it was the loss of safety and tenderness that she made up for. And so comprehensive were the attributes divined for her, so exhaustive the virtues posited for her, that nothing, no one, has been able to improve on her.

For these and so many other reasons, the Wife, that creature who gives only from her pure, loving heart and wants nothing for herself but to love and be loved in return—the heroine of the only love story we know and trust—has not been toppled, even if she appears to have fallen somewhat out of fashion. We may no longer aspire to such angelic goodness, just as we may not want to believe we will find her there at the altar, smiling sweetly and triumphantly.

But there she is, like the ghost of marriage past, challenging us to defy her. And we embrace her and take her in.

5

Marriage Shock

Marriage is an institution. I'm not ready for an
institution yet.

—MAE WEST

BARBARA, A JEWELER in Mary Gaitskill's 1988 short story "Connection," tries to explain to her old friend Susan why her twelve-year marriage has ended. She says it isn't that she and John didn't know each other very well, nor that she doesn't love John anymore. "I'm not sure how to describe it," she says. "It was like everything that supported the relationship was coming from the outside." Even worse, she says, "it seemed as if our most intimate conversations were based on what we were supposed to be saying, and what we were supposed to be. Nothing seemed to come directly from us."

The first moment a new wife feels this odd remove—her words not coming from her own soul, her real life suddenly clashing with the expectation of what that life is supposed to be—that is a moment I call marriage shock. Like Barbara, a woman may first experience marriage shock simply as a conflict between two voices, her own and one that is not hers—like a crossed wire suddenly cutting into, and cutting off, a private phone conversation.

The voice eerily powerful enough to compete with her own belongs to the historical presence I've called the Witness, who immediately introduces her to her nemesis, the idealized, perfect Wife. Now *this* is the woman who fits into marriage, it suggests; *you* will have to fix yourself to be like her. The voice has force and moral authority, and in urging her to change herself to more closely resemble a more attractive, "feminine," and nurturant cultural ideal, this condemning voice—actually an ancient chorus of voices all singing a single chord about women's conduct—produces profound emotional discord in our bride.

The curious split between who she is and who she is told to be, between what she really sees and knows and feels and wants to say and what she senses she should know and see and feel and say if she wants a happy marriage, is the experience of marriage shock. The Witness objectifies and judges her, silences her own strong feelings and thoughts as surely as any conduct-book author or fiery preacher back in 1800. And just as they did, it informs her about married love and about how she must behave to ensure it. The one love lesson the Witness is hell-bent on teaching is the virtue of selflessness and the evils of its dreaded opposite, selfishness.

The new wife is susceptible to the Witness and its strict "love" lesson at this particular juncture for a couple of reasons, one having to do with the way the psyche works. The psyche, psychologist Elizabeth Debold reminds us, is "not a thing, like the brain," but rather "a dynamic process that is in constant dialogue with parts of itself and with others," always taking in messages, attempting to figure out what is going on, struggling to orient us, develop answers, present choices about how best to proceed. "Its job is self-protection," she says.

The Witness's dominant voice—so sure, so right—makes even the most assertive and self-possessed bride hesitant about her own authority, even the most competent and confident woman tentative about where she stands on this selflessness-selfishness high wire. The most powerful, strongest, most mature women I know are perched up there as precariously as the youngest and most inexperienced brides, saying to themselves, "Look out!," wondering, "Am I doing this right? Am I headed toward a wonderful marriage? If I fall, will I still be loved?"

Her one hedge against falling seems to be the Wife's goodness, for the psyche responds to loss or the threat of loss by idealizing whatever or whomever might come to the rescue. Like the child whose parents have divorced and who idolizes the parent she isn't living with, the one she has "lost"; like the man ambivalent about a woman until she leaves, forever after pining for "the one that got away"; we tend to idealize what slips through our hands, imbuing that person or thing with the singular power to make us happy. The Wife, who seems to possess—to have and to hold—the relationship of our dreams because of her goodness, becomes the thing that can protect us from the danger of winding up alone. All we have to do is follow her lead.

Because the Witness's judgments about feminine goodness, truth, and value have gathered momentum for nearly three hundred years and resonate similar messages about goodness women hear throughout their lives, and because, most of all, *a great marriage* is what this goodness guarantees, they carry with them a historical weight and power that quite simply overrules a woman's own personal strivings.

If this ideal marriage gets her attention, the ideal Wife—that imaginary woman out there somewhere who does it all wonderfully, this business of loving and being loved, and who has a fabulous marriage to show for it—is what haunts her. The urge to become her, to become perfect, is simply the urge to believe that marriage can last, that it's possible to behave in such a way that she won't lose her marriage. The danger of being alone, of blowing it, of becoming one of those terrible divorce statistics, creates in her a psychic watchfulness, a hair-trigger receptivity to the words of someone, anyone, who will protect her from that unbearable loss.

So the Witness, with its seductive promise and its dire warnings, is not someone she's likely to ignore.

ALTHOUGH MEN WANT a wonderful marriage just as much as women do, a husband is less likely to walk this same tightrope of concern, to feel marriage shock in the same way. Men are not socialized to *idealize* either marriage or their own roles within it, so their expectations, of marriage and of themselves, are not the same. They aren't encouraged to make marriage the center of their lives; nor are they taught to become the emotional guardians of that marriage. They are neither encouraged to see a conflict between their own pleasure and pleasing others, nor to perceive these two disparate sensations as inextricable or, worse, synonymous. They are not expected to give up their needs and desires when they marry (although they may) in the interest of being good husbands; it is assumed that a man may be self-nurturing and find pleasure and fulfillment outside his

family without compromising the well-being of his family or im-
pugning his role as a good husband or father. (This is not to say
a man doesn't wish to have more time with his family, only that
he isn't considered "selfish" or a bad husband for pursuing his
own personal goals while also attending to his family.)

Married men, then, are less likely than wives to be hurled into
the center of the selfishness-selflessness dilemma. They are less
likely to assume that their behavior is the crucial determinant of
their marriage's success or to believe that the tenor of their marriage is established solely by them. There are many reasons why
wives and husbands respond to marriage and to each other differently (sociologist Jessie Bernard first observed the existence
of "his" and "her" marriages, with each spouse answering questions about the "facts" of their own marriage so differently they
appeared to be different relationships entirely), some rooted in
their different use of language, some in their different experience of the same event, some in their different place in society.
A man's social status, for example, is neither raised nor lowered
by marrying, nor is marriage expected to transform him, to
change his goals for himself or to alter his very essence somehow.

AT FIRST, THE voice of the Witness produces one particular kind
of self-alienation, that odd sensation gripping Gaitskill's heroine that "nothing comes directly" from her, and that leaves her
feeling as if candid, intimate communication with her husband
is somehow cut off.

Rita, newly married at the age of thirty-seven, further amplifies the sensation: "It's as if someone is always listening, as if what
I say and do is being taped, and could be played back any sec-

ond, as proof of—what? My mettle, my worth. And when it's played back, *there it is,* how well or badly I'm doing as a wife, for everyone to observe—like a little mini–Judgment Day."

Rita is embarrassed by this split between what she says to her husband and what she feels she is supposed to say. Indeed, when she listens to the two voices warring inside her, arguing over her ideal versus her actual self, she feels "stupid," she says—"like, I mean, get a grip. I'm trying to talk to my husband like a normal person, and I keep having this sense of watching myself from someone *else's* point of view."

Psychoanalysts, referring to the complexity of our sexual desires, the persistence of Oedipal struggles in the adult psyche, tell us that there are always at least four people—both sets of parent figures—in bed with every couple: I have observed yet another person in the wife's new family: the Witness, representing the institution of marriage. It confronts our bride with the shocking news of this ancient icon, the Wife, whose praises it can't stop singing. The Wife is not an icon Rita admires or even accepts, but there that Wife is, as dated as a starched trousseau in a steamer trunk, as outmoded as a primer on Victorian table manners. And with her comes, like a sinister wedding gift, a list of the rules and regulations, like the bare bones of the institution, long buried but shining still, presented by the Witness, whose job it is to polish and preserve them. The Witness dictates prescriptions for wifely goodness; it acts as a messenger of traditional values on behalf of the culture, often against our husbands' will as well as our own.

Psychologist Dana Crowley Jack, observing an "inner dialogue" of two competing voices in clinically depressed women, calls the more judgmental voice "the Over-eye" because it hovers over and overrides the "I" of the woman's own real voice. Jack distinguishes the Over-eye from the conscience because it repeats and reinforces cultural injunctions that may have little or nothing to do with a woman's own deeply personal moral strivings. Similarly, the conduct the Witness prescribes restrains and contains a wife in a way that her own conscience does not, and the taboos it names far outnumber her personal ones.

Nor is the Witness's voice the superego. A wife's personal morality and her own internalized familial figures seem specifically irrelevant to the Witness; rather it "knows" in absolute and general terms how she should feel and think in order to maintain a relationship, "knows" how her marriage should proceed and how she should *be* in it if she wants to be loved; and it demands that she obey or else forfeit that love. But what *it* knows differs from what *she* knows; her own experience of relationships and her natural impulses tell her a different story from the one the Witness tells. The conduct it advises is not familiar; the morality being urged is not felt; none of the behavior is loving, or sexual, or fun, or funny, or *hers*.

Her knowledge comes from a physically grounded moral certainty originating deep within her belly; the voice of the Witness, by contrast, brings her strange news about marriage as a place where her conduct must change; surprising news, far removed from her experience of friendships and relationships, those messy, vital, imperfect involvements that she understands better than this ultimate one.

The Witness, however, does not seem concerned with the woman's feelings. Her pains, her fears, her desires, her losses, her successes, and her love are not factored into its message despite the fact that the behavior it prescribes is supposed to be good for her. The Witness's ability to sound so clear, objective, and right is resonant of the clinician's language in a medical textbook. Its authority is like that of bad psychiatry, which reduces complex experiences felt from within to labels applied from without. In her book, *Engendered Lives,* Ellyn Kaschak observes how the "pains and fears of human existence" are "flattened" when approached by traditional psychology and psychiatry: "The language of diagnosis is distant and often disapproving. Its perspective is external, its voice one of authority."

Because it does not concern itself with how a married woman is feeling, only with *how she is doing as a wife,* the Witness, like Jack's patriarchal Over-eye and Kaschak's "diagnosis," declares what is "good" and "right" and "healthy" for a woman by a standard external to her, and it condemns her own views as "bad," "unhealthy," and "improper" when they diverge from culturally expected "shoulds." Nor is the Witness concerned with anything—pleasure, knowledge, growth—that a woman might gain from her marriage, other than the safety, security, and sanctity traditionally promised her if she follows instructions. Interestingly, too, the only losses the Witness recognizes are those it threatens: the love and approval a woman will surely forfeit if she doesn't conduct herself according to its edicts. The Witness seems unaware of the losses she might already have experienced upon entering the institution, encountering its demands that she be better, and less, than herself.

The Witness is distinctly mute on the subject of a woman's developing her spirituality, her spontaneity, her unconventionality, her creativity, the medley of authentic strivings that spring from her deepest self and that sum up as her sexuality. In fact, the Witness actively discourages the wife from indulging in emotional or creative expression—which I believe are inseparable from sexuality—warning her constantly against seeking pleasure and fulfillment for herself lest she endanger her marriage. The Witness is concerned with how a wife's conduct betters the lives of those whom she is supposed to put first; putting *herself* first is precisely the behavior it calls "selfish" and ruinous to her relationships.

Women's experience of fighting off internalized charges of selfishness has been a theme in the work of psychologist Carol Gilligan, who observes a "doubling of voice" in adolescent girls; psychologist Natasha Mauthner sees the same phenomenon in women suffering from postpartum depression. But watch: It's at crucial junctures in their development—on the cusp of adolescence, at the moment of marriage, just after giving birth—that women are plunged into this drama of warring voices, one embodied and authentic, the other repeating social conventions and expectations.

As I said earlier, adolescence, marriage, and motherhood are all *sexual* rites of passage. Each is feted by society as a milestone of female sexual maturity, a triumph of womanly ripening, yet the girl's or woman's own experience is rarely so idyllic. Her tumultuous voice tends to be drowned out by society's celebratory chorus.

What she *can* sense is that the warring voices are fighting over her sexuality. At adolescence, her burgeoning power and desirousness smash into the wall of the culture's need to control them, and she is flattened.

One or two decades later she will come to the next intersection of female sexuality with the culture, and this now-grown-up woman will eagerly enter marriage, where the same invisible demands, the same hidden controls, threaten to flatten her all over again.

And at motherhood, of course, where the expectation of womanly perfection and selflessness reaches its peak, adding to women's own true desire to love, nurture, and give to their children, the Witness has a field day. As one of the women in Mauthner's study of postpartum depression said: "You know, you're *crucifying* yourself all the time. . . . When you're in the illness, everything is the end of the world—it's black and white, good and bad. 'You were bad, you didn't do the cooking right, you didn't socialize enough, you didn't make enough witty, sparkling conversation.' . . . As soon as someone's gone, you're saying to yourself, 'You're bad, you're bad, you didn't do this, you didn't do that,' but why, why do you do this?"

Another mother, Sonya, said the voices would "carry on . . . in my mind, saying, 'If you'd been more relaxed, this wouldn't have happened. If you'd taken each day as it came, and didn't worry if Suzie made a mess, it wouldn't have happened.' "

Women experiencing postpartum depression speak of being "weighed down by all these stupid thoughts going through my mind," of how "even when you close your eyes, it doesn't go away . . . you can't escape it." One woman, Petra, perceives her struggle "as if you've been got by the devil . . . dragging you down, and he was winning, and you'd be fighting it . . . and yet he would always win, and he'd be taking over your whole body, and it's like you were being sort of *possessed* somehow, and this whole thing was taking you over and you were fighting like mad."

In single life, the interior voice of women's knowing, like a soprano solo, is strong enough to resist domination; single life is unprecedented, ungoverned, free space; there may be a behavioral debate about etiquette, but essentially the culture is disinterested in her life when no men or children are in it, so she may express herself as she wishes. But, once a woman marries, this free, resonant voice is precisely what is called into question, outsung by the voice of the Witness. Suddenly challenging these grounded, sure, and embodied feelings, the Witness, expert on the strange new territory she has just entered, undoes her authenticity as a knowing woman, much as girls lose their sassy certainty the moment they enter the treacherous terrain of adolescence. Her personal authority and knowledge are precisely what a woman so often feels being mysteriously undermined once she marries, even though she isn't sure why or how, even when she knows it is not her husband who is responsible. Her authority, her agency, her conviction just seem to "give way," as Amanda, newly married at forty-two, puts it, "because what I'm used to doing and saying seems out of place, even inappropriate, here."

What seems more appropriate, she says, "is to go along with whatever it is that will take me to that romantic place in my head, to the marriage I think I want." That "something else" in her leaves her own feelings of how to conduct her life suddenly groundless, as "I find myself questioning the idea of going after what I want by reminding myself that I already *have* what I want now and, well, that I should not want a whole lot more; that there's a price of 'having it all' and that it's a crass and ugly thing to want anyway."

"Are you speaking about wanting more materially?" I ask her.

"Yes, materially, but also emotionally, spiritually. Something clicked in when I married that says, 'Now keep it good. Don't push. Don't ask for too much, sexually, monetarily, whatever.

Don't be too *needy,* too dependent, too grasping. Don't go after too much. Don't surprise or disappoint or alarm him. Keep this thing you want so much really, really good.' "

"And the way to keep this thing really good is to stop being yourself somehow?"

"There's this voice in me, see, that wants me to keep things on track, to keep our love alive. And that means I have to be careful, to monitor myself—I don't want to be too needy, but I don't want to hide my needs, either."

"But either way, you're doing a balancing act; you must be eternally vigilant."

"Yeah, because I'm the one with the power to keep the relationship strong."

"And it will be strong as long as you aren't—too *you?*"

"Yeah." She laughs and catches my eye, as we both hear the words. "Right. I know. It's ridiculous. I can have a fantastic marriage as long as I'm not too me."

Amanda knows, of course—she just said so—that there is irony in the very idea of a "fantastic relationship" that excludes her as she really is. She knows, too, that her husband would be horrified at such an emotional arrangement; that he is as aware as she that any relationship between two people that is dependent on only one to "keep it really good" is "a little weird." He *wants* her to speak up the way she always has. He *wants* her to be the same sexy, outspoken woman he married. He, like most husbands, *wants* the woman he married, not some other woman, whose ear is tuned to the Witness's rules. And yet she only knows that she wants this relationship more than anything and that, if keeping her marriage good is her job, her responsibility, then so be it.

Once again, it may seem as if I am downplaying men's role in sending the good-woman message to their wives. Whether individual men sound like the Witness or not, it's important to see that the Witness and the man are not identical. A wife's dynamic with the Witness is separate from her relationship with her husband, even if at times the messages she receives from each are remarkably similar. Sometimes the Witness amplifies what the individual man might say (particularly when he says, "Where's dinner?" or in some way reinforces the demands of the role of wife), but even when it speaks through men, it is not the same as the man. When the Witness gets confused with the individual man, he gets blamed for an institutional position he may indeed sometimes channel and benefit from but also sometimes hate and be bewildered by. To the extent that he plays along with the Witness, he gains control and freedom to pursue his ambitions, but he winds up with a lot of selfless service from someone who's not there anymore—thereby gaining the Wife but eventually losing *his* wife, the woman he loved. Divorce statistics bear out his loss.

The power of the Witness and its litany of instructions, all of which speak to her of monitoring herself, of containing or constraining herself so as to have this "fantastic relationship," wins out over the strength of her own knowledge and over another, more fluid and forgiving story of love, a less careful one, a more prosaic, free-flowing, and pleasurable one—a new story more *lived* than *told*—a process still sketchy and lacking a collective voice to authorize it. The Witness's language of oughts and shoulds is punitive, not a forgiving discourse of desire, love, or friendship; it is a language of dualities, of good and bad, right and wrong, men and women, win and lose.

Listening to the Witness lecture her on how to maintain a re-lationship or else forfeit it, Rita comes to believe that what she is hearing is not merely a voice, but the truth. Because that voice speaks of a world she is just entering and of which she has enor-mous expectations and hopes, she is willing to listen, to follow the dictum of one who knows the way better than she does, and, by superimposing it over her own hesitant story of love, to con-cede altogether to the voice that seems to know best.

As her own voice grows fainter next to that gospel-like cer-tainty, she begins to lose track of her own feelings, any feelings that don't pertain to the good Wife and her tireless concern for others. Sensing that they are unwelcome in this new territory, Rita begins to call such feelings "selfish" and "bad," just the way the Witness does. As she bows to a more august relationship ex-pert, she devalues her own expertise; and the less she hears her-self articulate her own gut knowledge, the more she loses touch with it and the more dependent she becomes on the Witness to tell her how to "do" the relationship right.

There is a problem, however: The marriage advice the Wit-ness offers has little to do with her and her husband. It provides no information about *her* unique relationship, only about the preservation of the institution. What she cares about is connec-tion, closeness, love; what *it* cares about is goodness, specifically, *her* goodness, as a means of maintaining a marriage. It holds out "a good relationship" as its reward for her goodness but threat-ens her with the loss of her husband's love, her marriage, and social approval if she falters. But if she succeeds, too, she loses, for like a jumper cable attached to only one car's battery, the "connection" cannot be real when it is unplugged and left dan-gling at one end.

The notion of self-sacrifice as women's true nature is embedded within the institution of marriage as invisibly and as inextricably as DNA in cells. The Witness, embodying the voices of our forefathers and mothers, our poets and pastors, our authors and historians and presidents, still insinuates the characteristics of the Wife, like vials of poison, into women's ears. Women describe their attempts to resist: "I battled it" and "I fought like hell"; but then "I made myself do it" and "I always end up punishing myself." In the end, they buckle under: "I kept fighting until I seemed to just be fighting *myself*"; "I just figured, screw it, I'll do it according to the book"; "Hey, my mother did it this way, so it can't be all wrong." And as a result, what could be an intensely pleasurable story of love becomes instead a story of betrayal.

The Witness, I want to emphasize, is a part of the psyche that repeats cultural scripts; no one can be blamed for its existence or for its murmurings. Through it, a whole world of knowledge is passed down as surely by our mothers and grandmothers as by our fathers and grandfathers. It is, I think, diversionary at this point to assign gender to the Witness, because whether a wife hears a male or a female voice in this institutional recording—whether we deem it patriarchal, misogynist, or masculinist, religious or secular—the Witness is so deeply embedded in middle-class culture as to live in us all by now, its promptings masquerading as messages from our own souls, hot-wired to our nerve endings.

The Witness begins to exert psychological pressure on wives immediately, right at the wedding or sometimes even earlier, in the preparations for it, certainly once the word *marriage* has become final. Its purpose is to guard the institution, to protect the status quo, to ensure the continuation of marriage as we know it, and its function is to control women's conduct, to drum into us word of that specific "morality" created at the same time as separate spheres were born. The Witness loves to invoke the romantic myth as bait, always holding out the seductive promise of perfect love, and it loves the mute heroine of that story. It is no champion of women's rights, the Witness. And it is oblivious to the men and women who are. It speaks not on individual couples' behalf, but on behalf of the institution, like a sergeant barking the rules of the army, or a mother superior declaiming the dogma of her sect. The Witness is the voice of three centuries of authority, preaching a hellfire sermon about how to save and lose love.

Marriage shock marks the moment of suddenly knowing you have to listen.

And how does a woman react to this shock, this sudden blow to all she knows and is, this alien yet imperative set of survival instructions? Like a young marine who finds himself with his head shaved and a sergeant yelling in his face that he'd better forget all he knows and feels if he wants to *be a man,* our new bride is stunned, split between the role of a numb, obedient new recruit stumbling through the unfamiliar rules and a forbidden, spontaneous self that "plays dead" lest it make her slip up in this new high-stakes game.

Unlike the marine, however, the new wife is alone, isolated from fellow "recruits" with whom she might band together to secretly mock and resist their tormentor, a tormentor who, moreover, is invisible, not an obvious oppressor or acknowledged figure of fun embodying the institution. There is no one to validate the wife's own protesting feelings or to take her side when the voice of the Witness in her own mind tells her those feelings are wrong or bad. Instead, she steps into the fold of other wives, who are under the same pressure she is not to protest. She's not alone, exactly, she's *in the culture;* her greatest anxiety—being accepted into the Wifehood Club—has been relieved, and a core need for social approval has been met. But the knotty dilemma is this: This need for acceptance and normalcy, once gratified, eases her anxiety at the same time that it prevents her from questioning her sacrifice or even recognizing it.

As at adolescence, and at new motherhood—the other two times when a woman's sexuality is under scrutiny and conscripted into service, her real feelings written out of the script—the new wife is severed from her authentic self, and then, immersed in celebration, forbidden to acknowledge her loss and anger. And when loss is denied, when anger is repressed, they fester into depression.

Shock, after all, is defined as a "state of profound depression of vital processes resulting from wounds." We would never think of a new bride as being wounded, and neither would she. Yet, just when she is supposed to be feeling completed and fulfilled, she is experiencing a shutting down of vital feelings—the classic response to trauma. Sadly, ironically, in the moment of pledging herself to an ideal she has lost precisely what she thought she was securing: relationship—the imperfect, nourishing connection between people as they really are, and the affirmation of our real self that we all seek in love.

6

Reverberations

In the staring gas light, the women, throwing back their
shawls from their dishevelled hair revealed faces which,
though dissimilar in features, had a similarity of
expression common, typical, of all the married women
around and about; their badge of marriage, as it were. . . .
a married woman could be distinguished from a single by
a glance at her facial expression. Marriage scored on their
faces a kind of preoccupied, faded, lack-lustre air as
though they were constantly being plagued by some
problem. As they were.

—GEORGE ELIOT
The Mill on the Floss

SEVERAL YEARS AGO, after reading in repeated studies that
women were having affairs earlier in their marriages, and for
reasons no one seemed to understand, I decided to explore the
world of women's (and men's, obviously) adultery. I had stacks
of letters from young women as a result of my column in *Mademoiselle,* called "The Intelligent Woman's Guide to Sex," and I
found that their words supported the findings: They were having affairs early, startlingly so.

In 1992, my book *The Erotic Silence of the American Wife* was published. The response to it was dramatic. Some people, fascinated by what women said about marriage and extramarital sex, praised my effort; others were filled with rage—not only toward any woman who would stray from the sanctified marriage structure, but toward me, as the messenger of their experience. I was called a "witch" by a man on *Larry King Live* who thought I was leading faithful wives astray by even discussing the actions and feelings of their wayward sisters. More bizarre, because less overtly crankish, Barbara Probst Solomon wrote a lengthy editorial on the op-ed page of *The New York Times* (July 9, 1992) not only accusing me of advocating adultery, but taking exception to women's sexuality as a legitimate subject for me to write about or focus on, "as if this and not economic security is the crucial problem for American women," she said. It apparently wasn't clear to her that had I wanted to write about money I would have. Her real point, like the man's who called me a witch, was that discussions of women's sexuality—whether that sexuality is expressed inside *or* outside of marriage, I would guess—should be silenced.

One retail chain agreed. The book buyer for K mart refused to carry the book because of the word *erotic* in its title. He decided—by his own admission, without reading it—that it must be a "dirty book" and not something he would want wives exposed to.

Although I was stunned and angry, I was also oddly pleased by this perfect illustration of the book's thesis: the literal silencing of *erotic* for wives, the cultural inclination to muffle talk about women's pleasure. I took it as further evidence that what I was on to was right: Men's adultery isn't scary ("Why Men Cheat" is a timeworn favorite on magazine covers and talk shows), *women's* is. Men's erotic pleasure isn't scary (think D. H. Lawrence or Philip Roth), but women's is. What these people were angry about, it turns out, is not adultery, but pleasure. Women's pleasure. In marriage or out of it.

CONNIE, A CLINICAL psychologist at a prestigious New England university, had long been mystified at her unhappiness throughout her twelve-year marriage, but for years she could not locate precisely why she felt so lost.

It was well after her divorce that she and I met, but not too long after she had begun to understand: "For so many years I felt unable to find a language in which to articulate my feelings and desires," she says. "Every time I tried to argue or to say what I felt, my lawyer husband added it all up and presented it back to me in lawyerese, and I finally just gave up trying to say what I felt, for what I felt was nonexistent in his language, and I could not find a language in which to make him understand me."

Now forty and the mother of two teenage girls, Connie has a soft, sure voice, with a hint of a southern accent, just barely enough of a drawl to make you lean in and listen to the idiosyncratic rhythm that promises a dry and self-deprecating ending. Her sly humor and flat, comic delivery make me laugh; but she makes it clear that all the humor and all the words available to her in the language—and the vast, rich language of feeling *is* her language, professionally—no matter how well or charmingly put together, cannot guarantee communication.

Connie's inability to find a language in which to speak to her husband so that he could understand her feelings and desires—understand *her*—is a dilemma often seen in couples' therapy:

Couples most often cite just this, "a communication problem," as their reason for seeking counseling—which roughly five million couples did last year in the offices of family therapists alone. I tell Connie I had been startled, before starting my own column in *Mademoiselle,* by the sheer quantity of material focused on "communication": "Try again," the advice went, time and again, when a woman wrote in saying she failed to get her meaning across to her man. "Try new words. *Male* words. Say it differently. Try a more *active* vocabulary, maybe use a *sports* metaphor (like maybe, 'Honey, you're out in left field, you know? I feel as if you're dropping the ball here, dear . . .')." The implication is, of course, that a woman's meaning, not only her vocabulary, is a foul ball or a wild pitch, out in left field, uncatchable. Or, worse, that women aren't even playing in the same ballpark.

Connie smiles. "The harder I tried to use his words, no, the harder I tried to please him—the more specific and emphatic I got—the dumber I sounded. The more I ended my sentences with question marks. And there wasn't a sentence in my own language that he would understand," she says, "so I gave up on words."

Mired in that murky, inarticulate world of feeling where women are so often accused of dwelling, if not wallowing, Connie finally went under, awash in the sense that her need for connection was doomed and that this "communication problem" was entirely her fault. Her loss of self in this love, she came to understand, had been signaled by her loss of voice.

THE MEN CONNIE dated after her divorce were, not surprisingly, less aggressive, less argumentative, less inclined than her former husband to use their rational verbal skills to obscure her feelings or their own. She was determined to find men she could talk to; she chose the ones who could hear her, who could respond to her needs and desires and not recoil from them as excessive, incomprehensible, or overly emotional, men whose vocabulary wasn't somehow more impressive, more technical, or more authoritative than her own. "I couldn't figure out why I was dating younger men all the time," she says. "And then I realized something that startled me: *I* was younger. All those years I didn't speak up, I also didn't develop. As a woman, as a person, I had sort of ossified. I was stuck at age, oh, I don't know, twenty-four or thirty-one or something, developmentally. I wasn't the forty-year-old woman I was in every other way."

Connie's insight that the silencing of her voice had everything to do with the stunting of her development is confirmed by developmental psychologists, who agree that the voice is not separate from the person but develops in tandem with it. Mary Belenky and her colleagues, authors of *Women's Way of Knowing,* observed at the end of their study that the voice "can be seen *as* the self" (emphasis mine).

> What we had not anticipated was that "voice" was more than an academic shorthand for a person's point of view . . . that it is a metaphor that can apply to many aspects of women's experience and development. In describing their lives, women commonly talked about voice and silence: "speaking up," "speaking out," "being silenced," "not being heard," "really listening," "really talking," . . . and so on in an endless variety of connotations all having to do with sense of mind, self-worth, and feelings of isolation from or connection to others. We found that women repeatedly used the metaphor of voice to

depict their intellectual and ethical development, and that the development of a sense of voice, mind, and self were intricately intertwined.

How does a confident, outspoken woman, not inclined to edit herself, one who may have spent years in therapy overcoming such inhibition, and years in relationships insisting on being heard, first come to feel she is "losing herself," and how does losing herself begin the slow erosion in her relationship with the husband she loves? What are the first signs that this relationship is being compromised and potentially disrupted? When women listen to the Witness in order to have their relationship, they find themselves on a different path, one that leads them away from it. Let's listen to these women as they try everything they can to hang on to a relationship that, because of the Witness so entrenched in their heads that they can't hear or see, has already been lost.

Here is how some women who later speak of "losing themselves" describe what happened in the early days of their marriages. Listen for images of voice in the words of Adele, Heather, and Clara, specifically for their characterizations of *the way* they spoke:

> *Adele:* I found myself doing this thing I do only when I'm nervous or with strangers; and I began doing it pretty much the day after we decided to get married. Something changed in the way I talked to him. I became more polite. Like, my voice got more, I don't know, cautious? Cheerful, reassuring.

Trying to be the perfect and loving Wife, she's become unknown to herself and estranged from herself and her husband. She's not *in* the relationship anymore.

Heather: I loved him so much and felt so amazingly committed to this. . . . I, like, monitored my words a little so we would get along really really well. Now, he wanted to get married as much as I did—in fact he was the one who pushed for it. And yet it was as if there was now an understanding that I had got what I wanted and in exchange for getting what I wanted, if I wanted to keep things good between us, I had better toe the mark. You have to understand, no one said this. This was how I was acting; it was as if we agreed on something, but we never were so crass as to say it. I was so shaky when I tried to talk about it. Neither of us would have even been able to pinpoint it, so I kept it to myself.

Adele and Heather, dazzlingly committed to their marriages, deeply in love with their husbands, are losing the relationship they had as they struggle with monitoring their words a little, and getting along really well. These tiny chinks in authenticity are sufficient to cloud over what they really feel and who they really are. In time this process is the reason they become unknown to themselves and their partners.

Clara: The first thing I did after we were married was to put off going to med school until we had fixed up our new place and settled in. I was only going to put it off one semester. But then it all seemed to work so smoothly, and I thought, well, one more term. And then by that summer, when I began thinking about starting school again, I found myself stuttering a bit when I brought it up, as if I wasn't supposed to or had forfeited the right, just a little, you know? I felt I had to answer to certain things—like how would the cats get fed every day and how would things run the way we were now used to having them run and, well, like those were my jobs and if I wanted any other, I'd better see to it that they—oh, you know. So I kept it [my thoughts about going back to school] to myself until I could be very confident and very focused. I hated feeling like we were some Victorian couple and I was asking for the moon.

I keep hearing images of inhibition and faltering, of "stuttering" and "holding it in" and "keeping it to myself" and becoming "shaky" as women describe their early struggles to hold on to their own needs and wishes while at the same time keeping their marriages solid—as though there were an inherent tension between the two. Clara, twenty-four, recalling how hard she tried to push through her reluctance to speak up about returning to school, shows how images of faltering soon became images of silencing.

I couldn't stand my own reticence. After all, we'd made a deal ages before. But see, I knew that going back to school meant two other things that made the deal uncomfortable for me now: that we—he—would have to pay for it, and that we'd be putting off having a child. So here I am asking for a lifestyle that felt like we'd be going backward monetarily and emotionally, living like two grad students rather than two adults with children, at the same time as I was suggesting that what we had wasn't good enough—and I just felt really selfish and sort of weird asking for it. At the same time, though, I was annoyed that he didn't make it easier for me, you know, say, "Hey, now, don't go back on your goals here, remember what you wanted! It's time to go get it."

So now there were two things I wasn't saying: one, how much I wanted to go back to school, and two, how irritated I was at him for making it so hard to talk about. Oh, and *three*, I

felt like I was doing something wrong, being self-centered or
unfair or something, asking for something I didn't deserve
and hurting him by doing so. As I was losing ground I was saying, why the hell are his *feelings* involved in my schooling, anyway?

Clara finds it hard to tell the truth outright, to say what really
feels right to her, assert what she wants: "I'm going back to
school." Her natural impulse to insist they honor the deal they
made that she go back to school because she *wants* to now comes
up against her equally strong desire to be "fair" and not "self-
centered" by considering her husband's desires as seriously as
her own. To do, in other words, what she feels she should do; to
compromise. Increasingly, her struggle is characterized by a fear
of conflict and of appearing selfish and demanding. Sticking to
her own announced plans has now mutated into "asking for
something I didn't deserve."

Suddenly Clara sees, from some other perspective she cannot
name except to say it's how "everyone else I knew saw things,"
that her own honest voice is "losing ground," beginning to
sound unpleasantly demanding. She is split now. One part of
her *knows* she has the right to school *and* marriage, knows that
they are not mutually exclusive and that it is "absurd" to pit one
against the other; the other chides that to leave the house empty
and the cats unfed and the child delayed and their income de-
pleted would be "doing something wrong" in the eyes of others,
making their marriage "move backward" according to some unwritten but fixed timetable. This latter presence judges her,
dominates, becoming increasingly righteous and condemning
as the voice that represents her desires begins to wane.

Her question—go back to school or get a job?—thus has shifted from a practical issue to a moral one, from working things out to the mutual satisfaction of both partners to one measured by a standard of what is "right and proper." Keeping quiet and getting work becomes the morally "right" choice because it hurts no one (*except her*), adds to the family income, and doesn't upset the marital status quo. She concludes, "You can't argue with a husband's hurt feelings," but a dwindling voice still protests, "Why the hell are his *feelings* involved in my schooling, anyway?"

The issue of whether *she* is hurt in this transaction is sinking under the heavy charge of "selfishness." She stands by the Witness now in naming what is right and determining what she should do. By aligning with the Witness, she steps away from and loses touch with herself, the very vibrant, serious, and sexy woman her husband loved, and, in a flash, undermines this relationship she found love in. Charles is the one who points this out to me, in a frenzy of bafflement and frustration: "She didn't want to go. That's what she said. She didn't want to go. But I didn't feel she was telling the truth. I kept saying, are you doing this because you want to or are you doing this for me or what? And I don't know, it always turned bad. I guess I should have just said, hey, you're going to school, *period*. But I felt that would be just the kind of thing that she would hate." In giving up what she wanted in order to cause no problems in the relationship, she basically lost what was so meaningful to her: school *and* relationship.

The entire debate, to school or not to school, is going on inside her head; it is an "argument" between her and the Witness, over her behavior, the shoulds and shouldn'ts, the goods and bads, the rights and wrongs of it. She feels unable to bring the debate outside her head and into a discussion with Charles, so that both she and he might hammer it out together, openly expressing what each feels, *both fully present in this relationship that they loved*. They've lost it, though, with her partiality to the Witness. Rather, she experiences a division between her inner world, in which she is deadlocked with the Witness, and the outer world, in which she increasingly senses she must present a more upbeat, conciliatory self.

Although Clara seems alone in this, she is not crazy. Her husband has made himself clear: He would prefer her to get a job, to try to get pregnant—but he will support her if she insists on going back to school. Although he isn't being what could be called "supportive," he hasn't refused to discuss it further, nor has he closed his mind. But from his wife's point of view, he has taken the position of the Witness—indeed, that position does suit him—but he is not stonewalling her or pressuring her. Their stalemate, she feels, is up to her to break, but she cannot find the courage, the stamina, or the assertiveness to do so.

Her fear of harming her marriage, of causing conflict, or of hurting or angering Charles by insisting on her own desires is precisely the fear she doesn't dare articulate to her husband, the fear that silences her. Her submission to the Witness in not burdening her husband with this upsetting discussion leaves her angry at him for "making me feel as if I were doing something wrong, asking for something I didn't deserve, and making it so hard to talk about."

And yet, she admits that he has had very little part in this drama, has not even been much of a participant in her internal battle, which is, after all, between her and the Witness. While she assumes her husband is on the side of the Witness ("making me feel like I'm doing something wrong"), she has little actual evidence for that. Fearful of voicing her feelings and causing trouble, she withdrew from the discussion first. And yet, having no knowledge that the Witness exists, she can only conclude that her husband, the only other apparent player in this terrible game, must be the one to blame for making her the loser.

I'm tracking the split between her actual and her idealized self so meticulously because the "communication problem" happens so fast that the nature of it, and the origin, are obscured: Who is speaking? Who is defending what, and why? She finds it impossible to ascertain that there is another secret player in this game besides her husband—the Witness—and a rival for both their affections: the Wife. It's crucial that we identify the Witness and the Wife as historical presences, to keep it clear that a wife's internal struggle is neither inevitable between men and women—the famous "war of the sexes" we think of as "normal" and unwinnable—nor "natural" between ego and superego. It is cultural. To make this point clear I've largely omitted men's voices from this book; I want to ensure that the voice of the Witness does not lose its specific nature, and that we don't become confused about the source of the message and the true origins of our power struggle.

Keeping the Witness and its message clear prevents us from confusing this unique struggle with a *relational* struggle in marriage; for it's not a relationship we have with the Witness. It's a one-way, authoritative lecture given us on the subject of our goodness.

Yet a wife so quickly becomes allied with the Witness in deciding what she can and cannot bring into her relationship, so reflexively and automatically withholds her own voice from her husband, that much of what she has to say is censored before they even begin to talk! As newly married women in record numbers flock to therapists who ask, "Have you *told* your husband you feel this way? Does he *know* you feel you can't speak to him? Can't you just tell him honestly what you feel?", the communication problem seems located within the marital relationship itself. But it is not.

The problem has already occurred long before a wife speaks to her husband. Her surrender to the Witness's judgments about what to say and not say has brought her to the brink of rage at her husband—the person she thinks she's doing it all for, the person she loves and doesn't want to hurt. It's a communication problem, all right, but *the communication that's problematic is coming from the Witness.*

Human relationships become more vital and more resilient through mutual, two-way interaction; the Witness actively obstructs this interaction. It blocks Clara's connection to her husband, curtails the possibility of mutuality *in advance* of any discussion with her partner, by devaluing and defeating her authentic voice *before her partner even hears it.* Only after this losing battle with the Witness does she revise her voice to sound more "good," then feels she must cover her distress at self-silencing by not seeming angry or hurt, lest *that* disrupt the relationship—a self-betrayal that makes her even angrier! Feeling false, she realizes that further falseness is necessary to "make this thing, this marriage, work."

In standing by the Witness's tale of what to do about school, a tale that is all about what the perfect Wife would do in her shoes, Clara has betrayed herself. And she knows it.

But she must pretend everything is just fine, lest she seem unhappy, ungrateful, or unwilling to compromise. By obeying the Witness and circumventing *its* definition of a communication problem, any kind of two-sided conflict at all, she has severed connection with her husband about her real feelings, turned a negotiable, practical problem into a nonnegotiable, moral one, and set in motion the huge and mystifying communication problem! And Charles, confused and angry that she has disappeared, has also disappeared!

Notice that she hears in the Witness's voice, and imagines others would concur, a host of reasons for directing her behavior, not one of which furthers her own best interests or desires. The authentic lone voice of her own desire, that embodied voice that feels right and true because it is grounded in her own intuition and knowledge, feels at odds with all the voices of others who matter to her, whom she imagines are allied with the Witness in advising her to give up this "selfish" plan and enjoy the marital fulfillment offered her in its place. By the time the Witness is through with her, that lone and increasingly tentative voice that is her own will be silenced. And the less she hears herself speak what is true for her, the deeper she slips into self-doubt about the truth's legitimacy. Not only does her actual voice lose ground; her own actual *feelings* go with it.

Clara wonders, briefly: If her needs are so opposed to the needs of her marriage, then what is marriage? But she silences those thoughts. The disappearance of this resisting voice surprises her.

I thought, this is *ridiculous*. I'm acting like a complete dodo. I pictured myself telling my old therapist that I was having trouble telling my husband that I was going to go back to school and seeing that look on her face, like, "Come again?" She would wonder, I know she would say, "What, have you become a bride of Islam? Have you taken intensive Stepford courses? Tell me what's happened to you that your four years of therapy have come to nothing! Tell me how it became your job and your job alone to take care of the cats and the plants? And who, pray tell, if you're not, is going to see to it that you get a life?"

Split enough now to require memories of her therapist's voice to speak for the increasingly secret part of her that she senses is going under, Clara talks of her desire to feel good about the framework she increasingly feels bad about—

as if I were being asked to choose between marriage and school but that both, together, were just—too much to ask. Now, of course, I would ask it, I would get there, this isn't 1950. But that wasn't how it felt: Any mention of school felt like a direct challenge to my marriage, to marriage itself—no, worse, a challenge of my love for my husband! Like, if you love him, if you love marriage, if you love your home, blah blah, you'll— what? You'll shut up! You'll shut up! You'll take care of those fucking cats! Really. I know this sounds like I'm making a big deal of this, and that the argument is so stupid, but that's how it felt. Now, you have to understand, it never occurred to me before that this would be an issue. Never. Charles and I met in school and this simply wasn't among the problems between us that I envisioned.

This is the iron framework of right and wrong, good and bad, inside which a woman begins to stutter, falter, cover over, and finally lose altogether the voice that was "true" to herself. She loses the voice that represents her, her real self; she understands that she's in a framework in which that real self is not as *valuable* as her idealized self. She has little choice but to swallow that true voice for now and join the chorus that endorses and exalts the framework of marriage.

> I finally just said, to hell with it. I'll go to night school. I just don't care that much at this point; it's not worth it. I can't feel angry all the time about stuff that I guess just shouldn't matter to me, and I'm not about to leave this marriage. So inside, I see myself as this wild woman who probably shouldn't be married or something and I wonder, I mean, I wonder whether it's just me. If I didn't dwell on it, would I calm down? So I act cheerful because I just can't put myself through it, and yet, I see more and more built-in inequity now, and I thought that was all gone.

As she decides, on such a deep level, that she "can handle" swallowing her authentic words more easily than her husband can handle hearing them, she even decides how she should *appear* as she is being so falsely brave and self-sacrificing. She must "act cheerful," by covering her false act with a false face, just as the Witness would have her do, and just as the conduct books instructed the selfless Wife to do. And so she edges slowly into the "compliant relatedness" Dana Crowley Jack tells us is common to women in clinical depression, a behavior designed to ensure relationship, but which instead severs it as cleanly as a saber.

As the Witness's voice successfully usurps her honest voice, and its do-good-to-others message obscures her desires, even the resonance of her supportive therapist's voice cannot help her stretch the walls of this framework, which suddenly feels to her like a trap, neither permeable nor pliable but deadly. Clara notices the change in her voice, how it's now "all sugary and pleasing, like that awful voice people use when speaking to children, too sweet and too anxious and, oh, you know, just fake."

She is horrified to find herself speaking in this falsely contented, "cheerful" voice, but she knows her own voice will betray her as the devious, rebellious radical she senses she really is. She becomes aware that speaking regularly in two quite different voices is essential if she wants to appear content in her marriage.

But that personal voice, although split off from the Wife voice, still lives. It is her private voice, not her public voice; it is used among close friends. It hasn't been completely silenced. Not yet.

"I HAVE RARELY met a woman in a conventional marriage," psychologist Carol Gilligan tells me, "who is not leading a double life in her relationship, who does not speak in this false voice in relationships."

The women I spoke with—mostly middle-class, loving wives all over America—hold those two voices inside, in a kind of dissonant harmony with which most women are all too familiar: one, a public voice, that sweet, good-woman voice in which we recite how fine we are, the well-adjusted voice of the Wife that other women recognize immediately as false; the other, a subversive voice we use with our closest friends, a voice that speaks from a secret self that knows what it feels and says what it means and doesn't give a damn about virtue.

Since feeling pleasure has become less vital to a wife's survival than *reporting* pleasure, testifying to the happily-ever-afterness of

marriage, the voice that speaks of her own real pleasure, her authentic voice (her erotic voice), is exiled out of earshot, deep-
sixed to a secret spot inside her, as if it were treacherous,
seditious. The voice that's most concerned with others' pleasure, and that calls her own desires and needs "selfish," is the
voice she now uses in her perfect-Wife conversations.

Her authentic self, that noisy, disruptive, and self-interested
being that longs to break out of the iron framework but doesn't
dare, is alone now, and she will henceforth reveal it only to her
women friends, if at all, but emphatically not to her husband,
thereby relegating him to the world of the Witness, unwittingly
casting him in the role of a critic who cannot hear or comprehend her, who will neither know nor accept her. And it isn't
true! He already did hear her, and knew her and loved her. And
he will remind her of that, when she asks again and again for re-
assurance and love: "I married you, didn't I?"

Whenever I hear that infamous dialogue: "Do you love me?"
and its reply, "Sure I do, I married you, didn't I?" I realize why
it's so common, and painful. A man is responding to his understanding of marriage as the consummation of a woman's desires; that by marrying her he has given her everything he could,
everything promised her by the fairy tales. But the words convey
his pain: *I loved the you I married. I loved who you were then, when we
married, and you knew it.* And her understanding of the truth of
this sentiment leaves her lamenting the loss of that woman and
still more unsure of whether *this* woman is loved. So she says, "I
know he loves me, but I don't *feel* it."

And then I see the Witness not just as a tired old taskmaster,
an old Saturn left over from centuries ago, but as a contempo-
rary and brutal mugger, robbing wives' selves and couples'

homes, stealing their love. And I'm reminded of what Lore Segal said recently, in a review of Jamaica Kincaid's *The Autobiography of My Mother*, about the cruelty of another ancient thief: "Colonialism steals a people's natural religion," she says, by forcing them "to believe in the gods of the people who had conquered them." Once the oppressed adopt their oppressor's view of themselves, she continues, a view designed to defeat them, "it incapacitates their affections. That is their defeat." The Witness, conqueror of wives, robs women and defeats them in precisely the same manner, by incapacitating their affections.

That self Clara wanted so to bring into the relationship, the loving self Charles, no doubt, fell in love with, is now lost to him as she dissembles in the name of love. A behavior designed to ensure relationship has, instead, simply ended it, even while the marriage lurches on.

7

Of Two Minds

"Ah yes!" returned Felicite. "You're like old Guerin's
daughter, the fisherman at Le Pollet, that I knew at
Dieppe before I came to you. . . . It seems she'd got a sort
of fog in her head, the doctors couldn't do a thing with
her, and no more could the *cure*. When she got it real bad
she'd go off by herself along the beach, and the
coastguard often used to find her there on his rounds.
Stretched flat out on the shingle she'd be, crying her eyes
out. . . . They say it went when she got married, though."

"But with me," replied Emma, "it didn't come on till I
was married."

—GUSTAVE FLAUBERT
Madame Bovary

"SEVERAL MONTHS AFTER my wedding, . . ." Leah Heidenrich, a
psychologist in Laguna Beach, California, writes, "I dreamt that
my sister had whitewashed my altar." In her journal entry on Jan-
uary 31, 1989, she writes:

She has painted the base and parts of the foundation white.
The paint is rubbery and sticky. I peel it off with trembling

hands. The altar is made of dark wood. I am so angry and crying in my sleep. I cannot imagine what she was thinking of. She stutters and peeps. I tell her I would like to tear the flesh from her face in little pieces and eat it.

This and other entries from Heidenrich's journal were incorporated into her master's thesis on depression in newlywed women, a thesis that originated when she began to try to understand the "deep depression" she herself fell into immediately following her wedding, a depression she knew was "an unacceptable response to one of life's most romanticized events."

"I felt guilty for questioning the inviolate happiness of the wedding," she says in her introduction, "guilty for being depressed; angry about something I could not begin to name."

What was she so angry about, she wondered. Why had she fallen into a depression precisely when she was supposed to be at her happiest? She interprets her dream, as the anger she felt at the denigration of the sacred ceremony of marriage in today's culture. A Jungian therapist, she felt she had unwittingly undergone a wedding that lacked the deep spiritual—dark—unity with the Other, her partner, the male. She lamented the fact that her own wedding, like so many others that focus on the external ceremony rather than the deeper meaning inside the ritual, had been stripped of symbolic meaning. "When an institution is reduced to the material," she writes, "when the preparations are stripped of symbolic meaning, depression is an understandable response to a rite which is ritual in form only, devoid of content."

The minute I saw the word *whitewashed* in Heidenrich's description of her dream, I felt there was a missing piece in her explanation of her own depression, some root cause that went beyond disappointment over the wedding ritual, beyond dashed expectations. I wondered about the darker, more violent feelings, that "anger about something" she felt so strongly but "couldn't begin to name." Was there more bubbling up in that dream of hers than that which she does name: the ceremony's having been "stripped of its symbolic meaning"? And was it sufficiently comprehensive to conclude that "depression may be the means by which the inner process is served in resolving the actual with the imagined"?

Hadn't she herself been feeling "whitewashed" since her wedding, her own dark feelings of rage, guilt, and confusion airbrushed first by the cultural obligation to feel wonderful when she didn't and later by a need to find some rightness, some normalcy, some inevitability, some *merit* even, in her and other women's depression at the altar?

I ask her.

"I *was* feeling whitewashed," she tells me. "The institution of marriage does whitewash the deeper feminine, by which I mean the sense of complete individuality that is part of being a woman." Her tactic, she explains, was to accept—or perhaps a better word is manage—her resulting depression. "Instead of allowing depression to be oppressive, psychologically and physically, I tried to work with it actively by turning inward," she says, adding, "I don't think of depression as a bad thing. We're such a happiness-oriented culture. Depression can be a resource if we follow it."

I agree with her that depression can have a positive outcome, and that investigating it can be valuable. But I feel, I tell her, that shifting our attention to depression as a condition that can be well handled or badly handled, positive or negative, begs the question of why so many women fall into a depression at this particular juncture, puts the burden on women to cope with it, resign themselves to it, rather than face the depths of it and look at what is wrong with the institution that causes such a condition. I am interested in the fact that she sees women's depressed reactions at marriage as "linked with an institution instrumental in the history of the devaluation of the feminine," yet what I sense is acceptance, not outrage at this spiritual injustice, and I miss her instinctive resistance to and protest against this devaluation.

How would that built-in "devaluation of the feminine" she observes make her—a woman, after all—*feel*? And doesn't the word *devalue* mean, in one of its definitions, "depress"? Shouldn't *that* emotion be investigated, felt? Was that perhaps the missing piece in her depression, her masked outrage turned inward? And I remember once again that in her book on depression in women, Dana Crowley Jack uses the word *devalue*— in fact, the same phrase Heidenrich does—interpreting the high rates of depression in women as "an almost inevitable response to living in a culture that deeply fears and *devalues the feminine* [emphasis mine]." And I remember, too, that the psychotherapist and body-image specialist Steven Levenkron explains the "distorted" perceptions suffered by so many American women not as body-image problems, but as a perfectly fitting resistance to seeing oneself reflected in the mirror of our culture's "antifemale ethic"—the thinness they're obsessed with reflecting what Naomi Wolf calls "not an obsession about female beauty but an obsession about female obedience." What they feel when they look in the mirror is *shame*, which "can be understood," Robert Karen observes, "as a wound in the self."

Whatever this depression so common to married women comprises, we must remember that the whitewashing job—diverting us from seeing and feeling our own pain and outrage—is what the Witness *does*. Squelching a woman's experience of how to be in a relationship, planting the idea that she must follow another script—that's the Witness's job. Sometimes we're alerted to it through dreams, sometimes by two conflicting voices—the authentic one and the Witness's—warring over right and wrong, good and bad, whether we're *handling* it well or poorly. Awake or asleep, the upshot is that women are split about who to be in marriages: We're *that* person, the good and cheerful spouse who doesn't notice signs of her own devaluation or depression or disorientation because we're told such feelings are impossible; and we're *this* person, I, me, the one who cannot be fooled, who takes it in, who knows what she knows even with her eyes shut. This double vision of reality—the one we're supposed to see (and the one we're supposed to *be*), and the one we know in our hearts is real—is what psychologists who listen to women are increasingly hearing as the very root of depression.

The Witness has another job, too: to so obscure the link between marriage and depression, to so discourage us from feeling it, that when we make that connection we feel more than guilt at having such an "unacceptable response," we feel shame. By urging us, just the way the conduct books did, to transform feeling bad into feeling good, it diverts us from our sensation of being whitewashed. "Much of the shame that therapists treat is repressed, defended against, *unfelt . . .* ," Robert Karen says in his article "Shame," in *The Atlantic Monthly* (February 1992).

And as I think about the way depression at marriage signals a loss we're not supposed to notice or feel, I am taken with another fact: that shame was itself first instilled, Robert Karen states, "as a result of the internalization of a contemptuous voice."

IN HER BOOK *Voice Lessons,* author Nancy Mairs tells us:

> The day I was married (actually, a few days beforehand since I got rather caught up in last-minute preparations), I stopped writing. These two events (one event and one nonevent, to be precise) might have been purely coincidental, but I suspect they weren't. Although thirty years later I can see that that day marked a beginning, which, like a healthy rootstick, has burgeoned over time into beginning after beginning after beginning, I had no such sense then. On that day something came to an end, something I might call my artistic youth.

It was 1963. Mairs was nineteen, and she had been writing for eleven years, poems and short stories "scribbled in time stolen from school assignments—the very opposite of dutiful, downright subversive of duty." Her abrupt decision to stop writing puzzled her:

> What was different about married life, I wonder, that made it resistant to subversion of this sort? Or—and I think this is the same question in different guise—what did I think writing was that my married state seemed to debar it?

Mairs decided that she had stopped writing because she had lost her father at the age of four, a loss that left her in such pain

that "what I needed above all else to fill that void was a man."
Once married, she believed, that pain of her childhood loss was
eased, so that she "had neither the motivation nor the material
to keep on writing." Acknowledging that her interpretation
might sound "far-fetched," Mairs tells her readers, "You'll just
have to take my word for it: once I was married, nothing in my
life seemed worth writing about."

And yet here, in her words, is what was going on in her life just
after she was married: "A final year of college. A brief, unhappy
stint of grade-school teaching. The birth of my daughter. An
episode of depression so debilitating as to require six months of
confinement in a state mental hospital."

Again, I was struck by Mairs's resistance to the possibility that
her marriage, more than simply the cure to her aching longing
for a man, might also be one cause of her aching loss of self; that
it was an event with emotional ramifications far beyond the joyful coupling she named it, a major ingredient in the soup of
emotions and happenings that fed her inability to write. Why
was her marriage *not* connected to a depression that struck her
down at that very moment? Why, when it marked the particular
day she ceased to write, is marriage neither implicated nor even
suspect?

And why would a passionate young writer conclude that she
"had nothing to write about" when the events following her wedding day were both so harrowing and so exciting they could
have filled several books?

Mairs does go on to answer these and many other questions
in a wonderful book that is all about the painful, exhilarating
process of filling this abyss with her own lost voice. But her
dilemma so brilliantly mimicked those of so many women that I

was struck once again by the irony: Just when women are supposed to have finally found true love, they're so often greeted with depression! Ironic but not accidental. And yet we continue to look everywhere but at this fact. Statistics tell the tale: Married women have a higher rate of depression than single women, than single men, than married men. *Much.* The connection between marriage and depression fills my research. Here's Jessie Bernard issuing the warning in 1972: "Marriage may be hazardous to women's health." The data have continued to pour in, confirming her words. I mentioned in Chapter One some of the research implicating marriage in women's depression—*marriage,* not genetics, PMS, birth-control pills, or even poverty. This finding has been publicized widely (Susan Faludi reported it in *Backlash;* I wrote of it in my last book), yet, says noted depression expert Ellen McGrath, M.D., the clear correlation between marriage and women's depression remains "psychology's dirty little secret." We all, it seems, suffer from the very denial Leah Heidenrich and Nancy Mairs did. None of us wants to make the connection.

Why are women so fearful of interfering with a system that puts their emotional well-being at risk, that is inhospitable to their real selves, that historically has no room for the whole beings, a system they so often want to leave? If any other social institution had a 65 percent failure rate, would we not agree that it was deeply flawed, that something about it needed fixing? If well over a half of all the people who happily entered the military, say, or the church, or our school system, walked out years before they had intended to, would we not investigate what they were running from? Would we not be as ready to discredit the values and vagaries of that institution as the integrity or morals of the dropouts? Yet, when it comes to marriage, we are looking out from inside the very framework that imprisons us, unable to clearly see the restrictiveness of the frame.

Similarly, what Heidenrich calls the "inviolate happiness of the wedding" is kept in place by the psychic split we discussed earlier, a split caused when the Witness steps in to encourage us to adhere to an imposed vision of marriage, a disembodied view of ourselves, and an external set of standards about conduct—a whole value system we then take on as our own. In this process of splitting, we become adept at seeing things as they "should" be through others' eyes. Through others' eyes, marriage confers upon a woman not only intimacy, identity, safety, and happiness, but an inner goodness, an acceptability, she didn't have before. Through others' eyes, marriage is the culmination of a woman's quest, the proof that she did it right, earned a sanctioned love, became the heroine of the story. Through others' eyes, marriage confers on her idealized qualities she didn't have before but could only dream of: "To love and be loved is to become a hero," British sociologist Annette Lawson reminds us. Through others' eyes, the vision of herself in this mythic condition of contentment is as resistant to questioning as the notion of happily ever after. A woman may "know" it is romanticized and unrealistic, "know" she herself views things differently, but even the children of divorce, even the oft-married and the most cynical about relationships, cling to the myth of the happiness of the married state and anticipate a happily-ever-after story for themselves.

If their story doesn't unfold as hoped (and does it ever?), they will opt to question not the narrative but themselves, for failing to become the heroines they should have been. Certainly where we find such intense denial, such a collective cover-up, there is something precious being threatened, some ingrained ideology or fantasy we are trying to defend. That so many women find it just as difficult as Mairs and Heidenrich did connecting their entry into marriage with the subsequent feelings of loss—in Mairs's case, a devastating inventory of losses—suggests that the process of excluding oneself from the relationship is either unnoticeable or too "unacceptable" to face. For many women, even to question the institution of marriage is to question their most important hopes and life choices. Even a question as mild as "Is there something about marriage that might not be hospitable to women?" can feel as threatening to some women (and many men) as "Are you, or have you ever been, a Communist?" once felt.

Because the myth of marriage is so sacrosanct, because to feel depressed at the crowning moment of one's life doesn't make sense, even women who set out to investigate the source of a depression look for it anywhere but in marriage itself. They would rather dismiss their depression as, say, a congenital debility, or some global female predisposition to the blues, or intolerance for happiness, or immaturity, chronic fatigue, hormones: anything so long as it doesn't challenge marriage. Nancy Mairs entered a union she "knew" would make her happy; how, then, could she "know," at the same time, a mysterious and crippling depression? No, such a response became unfathomable, unbelievable; it couldn't be written down because it was simply unspeakable.

AND YET WHEN women do speak, and we listen, we hear this unspeakable tale. There is a striking similarity, I've noticed, between the feelings women report in marriage and those they have when immersed in a clinical depression. If we begin tuning our ear to the idea of two voices in marriage, to the notion of the

Witness overruling the bride, we hear the very beginnings of what it feels like to be of two minds.

Beth, age thirty:

I don't know how to explain this, really, because I really love my husband and wouldn't want to be married to anyone else. But I have changed. Something in me is gone. It's vanished and I miss it and I don't know how to get it back.

Dorothy, forty-one:

This is my second marriage, and you'd think that I'd have learned whatever I needed to learn about why the last one didn't work. And I did, you know? But it doesn't seem to affect . . . this feeling I have that in marriage I can't keep myself completely whole. That it's not *compromise* we're talking about here, not *merging*, it's a sort of personality *amputation* I'm experiencing.

Alex, twenty-six:

About three months after I got married, I fell into a black hole, and when I came up out of it, there were whole parts of me missing, like both physical and emotional sensations that I've never gotten back. If that sounds dramatic, I can only tell you that the words can't fully convey how lost I felt.

Gayle, fifty:

I just think the truth is that if you put men and women together in a marriage, something happens to women that doesn't happen to men. They get smaller. Like that old play in which a woman "dwindles" into a wife. It even happened to crusty old me, and that is the least likely thing I could have imagined.

Linda, age twenty-four:

In the middle of all the wedding stuff, the ring, the dress, the cake, his mother and my mother and the china and hiring the hall, I felt, "I'm going under." It had nothing to do with the wedding, which in a certain way was fun, since I was doing the whole fantasy trip. It was something else. Little by little I was no longer me, and I felt like I was just going under.

The women I've spoken with consistently present this conundrum over the course of their marriages: How do I have marriage without going under? How can I keep both my marriage and myself? If I bring more of myself into my relationship, what will happen to my marriage? Can I still be me?

"Oh, no, what do I do now?" Addie, thirty-six, asked me quietly after she had told me the details of her marriage-onset depression, had listened to herself talk about it right here on tape, heard herself cry, "I want my marriage, but it feels split off from my love."

I realized as I was walking down the aisle that while something about me was now just fine and that I had gotten what I wanted, something was wrong, something was really wrong, that my life as I knew it was over, that . . . oh God . . . I was walking into something that I forgot to hold on to—no, that I actually put aside—like in a dream, where you forget to wear your clothes to a party or to study for an exam—something

about me, about keeping me alive, the me I never thought
until that moment was endangered.

Her passionate sense that she was "endangered" clashed with
her elation at getting married, and so, hoping the former was
just wedding jitters, she silenced her terror that her life as she
had known it "was over." Marie, president of a nonprofit women's organization, says she lay in the bathtub just before she
was going to get married and thought, "My life is over." Phyllis,
a lawyer, felt she "had come to the end of the world and was
about to fall off" when she married for the first time, the same
year Nancy Mairs did, in 1963, and wondered "what on earth I
was going to do *now*?" Well over fifty women have told me that
they knew something was very, very wrong *when they were walking
down the aisle*—not with the relationship, necessarily, but in the
stunning dissonance between what they were supposed to feel
and what they actually felt. They had the unmistakable sense
that life as they knew it was forever ending.

A thirty-two-year-old computer consultant from southern California said:

I wanted to stop right in the middle of the aisle and say,
"Hey, I forgot to negotiate something that's very very important here." Like some bargain I made that I really didn't in-
tend to keep, or some deal that didn't benefit me in any way.
It was incredibly weird. I felt I was being *compliant* somehow,
and in some way I would deeply regret.

Yup, I was walking down the aisle with my dad. And I turned
to him and I said, "Dad, this is weird, but I don't think this is
right for me. I feel *swallowed up*." What could the man say? He

squeezed my hand and said, "I'm afraid, darling, that we'll have to worry about it another time."

Stage fright notwithstanding, these women are using the same images—falling into an abyss or out of the world, with no way back—to describe a frightening sense of loss. Clinically depressed women use the words "loss of self" to describe the feeling of depression, and that is the precise image so many of my informants used to describe their experiences in marriage. It is useful, then, to examine why this painful metaphor, "loss of self," crops up in these two contexts; to see what similarities in a woman's experience of clinical depression and of marriage would prompt her to use the identical striking image. How does one "lose" one's "self"? What is the self, that it can be perceived as so diminished, misplaced, or attenuated that it can disappear? And why are these two seemingly different landscapes— depression and marriage—both potential quicksand for that self?

Clearly, I don't wish to suggest that marriage, *per se,* is tantamount to a clinical depression. On the contrary, love is a major reason married people stay healthier and live longer, and good health and happiness may encourage couples to marry. Rather, I want to search the two environments for common clues to the mourning for *being* that women experience in both. What is the "self" that women feel they are losing, and in what hostile terrain can it be lost?

Recent theories of women's psychology stress the idea that women's sense of self is deeply connected to others, that it is within and through relationships that we develop, thrive, and find our own voice and strength. Unlike the story of men's psychology, which moves toward separation and autonomy, women's psychological growth takes place in the rich nutrient medium of ongoing relationships. Our well-being is established and ensured by our connection with others at all stages of our lives. Unlike traditional psychological theories, which center on the development of a more separated sense of self, newer theories suggest that this self cannot be isolated from other selves. "We observe," says psychologist Jean Baker Miller, "that women tend to find satisfaction, pleasure, effectiveness and a sense of worth if they experience their life activities as arising from, and leading back into, a sense of connection with others." Women's sense of self thus "becomes very much organized around being able to make and then to maintain affiliation and relationships."

But there is a paradox in women's relationships that was observed at the same time almost a decade ago by psychologists Miller and Carol Gilligan, a paradox that accounts for some women's defeated efforts to maintain affiliation and connection. The "better" the self that women bring to their relationships, the more surely they take themselves out of those relationships. Certainly this is the very paradox these women reveal when they speak about their loss of self. But I'm hearing another, equally troubling new dimension to the paradox, one perhaps only visible in middle-class marriage. Precisely a woman's goodness, often considered her major qualification for marriage, separates her from her *sexuality*—her creativity, her self, her center—leaving her feeling increasingly numb and sexless with the very husband with whom she wants to share ecstasy. On the face of it, this makes no sense—marrying for delight and finding yourself cut off from it—until we remember that at the birth of the middle class, giving up sexuality was the essence of the conduct that declared a woman morally beyond reproach, and thus eligible for marriage in the first place.

To lose one's self, then, has a special sexual meaning for a wife. It suggests not only that her distinctive "I" is being overwhelmed, buried, or effaced within a relationship, but that *relationship itself*—her living connection to others—is being threatened or cut off. All the evidence suggests that it is when women feel threatened with the loss of connection that they are most likely to become depressed. According to the new relational perspective, which recognizes that human beings cannot thrive in isolation, "depression results from the inability to make or sustain supportive, authentic connection with a loved person," writes Jean Baker Miller. Maggie Scarf, too, found that it was "around attachment issues more than any other sorts of issues" that women's depressive episodes were most likely to occur. So why are women becoming depressed precisely *at marriage,* when they have supposedly attained the secure attachment and intimacy they have longed for? On the surface, this observation seems nonsensical, which is why women struggle to deny what they are feeling, working themselves deeper into the tar of alienation and loss.

The confusion clears up if we trust depression's signal and consider that the relationship *is* being threatened, connection *is* being severed, sexuality *is* being monitored, *right here* at the altar, where what we think we see is a man and a woman being joined together. What is really happening is that a woman's psyche is splitting so she's less in touch with her desires. And relationship itself is disappearing with that split, for relationship—as she knows, as she has lived it for years—is a messy, vital, contentious, sexual bond between two real people. An icon of empty goodness can't connect. At the moment she is officially gaining it all, the wife is in danger of losing everything—both aspects of herself—her relationship along with her sexuality, for they are inseparable. Women viscerally refuse to choose between their authentic sexual selves and their loving attachments, for to lose either one is also to lose the other, yet that is the choice the Witness demands she make. "Be yourself and lose love; be the Wife and win love." *This* is nonsensical.

How does a woman cope with these patently self-contradictory instructions? In the past, many women, under the strain of trying to do the impossible, literally went crazy. Today women have another option, one they resort to in ever-increasing numbers: They leave. I've said it before: 65 percent of all new marriages will end in divorce; close to three quarters of those divorces will be initiated by the woman. Not knowing what is wrong, she often blames the particular relationship and thinks the next one will be right—that the partner was the problem, not the institution. But second and third marriages end even more precipitously, and more often.

Knowing how important relationships are to women, this is a dramatic walkout strike, one that only makes sense when you realize that what women are blindly, instinctively protesting is *the absence of honest relationship in marriage.*

The Protection Racket

Tell all the Truth but tell it slant—
Success in Circuit lies
Too bright for our infirm Delight
The Truth's superb surprise
As Lightning to the Children eased
With explanation kind
The Truth must dazzle gradually
Or every man be blind—

—EMILY DICKINSON

I AM IN a town in suburban New Jersey with ten women, ages twenty-three to fifty-five, who meet once a month to discuss books. It is summer, and pitchers and glasses of iced tea dot the antique wicker tabletops like huge amber beads, the only jolts of color on this rambling, whitewashed porch. I am there to ask these wives about the early days of their marriages. I have spoken with them before, the first time in the summer of 1992, when they invited me to a discussion of my last book. There are a lawyer, a doctor, a psychiatrist, a political analyst, two social workers, a magazine advertising director, a painter, a stay-at-home mother, and a free-lance decorator, and they know what they are talking about; each has been married at least once and is currently married. They do not hesitate to speak openly in the group.

The books they have chosen for discussion in the past four or five meetings have tended to be titles they don't want to take home. "You know," explains the youngest of the group, Diane, aged twenty-three, "anything about women doing or feeling the opposite of what we're supposed to do and feel," which means, she adds, "anything about women's rage, power, adultery." Books on these and other subjects deemed "too difficult" to expose to questioning family members are saved for the group. I ask to hear more about what they call "paper-bag books," referring to the way men once carried around pornography in plain brown paper or bottles of gin in paper bags. Why is it that one title can go on a bedside table and another cannot?

How is it that women come to hide their own pleasurable activities from loved ones? I am interested in this odd and unquestioned duplicity that has infiltrated our married lives like dandelions in a flower patch.

I ask: Would you have felt any hesitation about sharing what you read with a man you were dating, or with your husband before you married him? That is, would you have felt you had to explain what you read or what you buy to any man who was not your husband?

"No," they all say in unison. And then there is laughter.

Magda, thirty-three, says, "When I was single, I read whatever I liked in front of anybody. I guess," she says thoughtfully, twisting a strand of her hair, "this really did start when I got married."

"Me too," says Ellen, twenty-nine. "When I first got married I used to hesitate to put the books I was reading down on the coffee table." When I ask her why, she says, "I think I thought I would be judged by what I was reading; like it revealed what kind of person I am or something."

"I discuss everything with my husband," Janet says.

Arlie thinks for a moment, then says she displayed books selectively when she first got married seven years ago, as a way of demonstrating her good taste, "the way, when you choose your china or crystal, you're saying to others, 'This is who we are as a couple; this is what our taste is, this is how we live, this is *us*.' Showing or not showing him what I read was like revealing only who I wanted him to think I am.

"But it was more than just about appearances, I think," she says softly. "During that Bobbitt case, remember? I found myself trying to make it so clear to Steve that I disapproved of Lorena Bobbitt, when I really didn't. In fact, I remember feeling, Good. Now maybe violent men will think twice. And I remember thinking, God, with all the things men have done to women, is this the first time that has happened? But I hid that truthful response. I knew what I was supposed to feel, though, whose story I was supposed to sympathize with. So suddenly here's this little voice that comes out of me saying how *crazy* she must be to do such a thing—like, if I were to admit any sympathy for her, I would instantly be called *anti-male* or something, a *radical feminist* or in some 'crazy' category myself."

Sherry says, "I always distance myself from women who break the law, killers or drug-takers or adulteresses, as if to announce to the world, 'Hey, I'd never do that! What a terrible woman! Kill her!' "

"I hated what I was doing, and I finally stopped doing it," Ellen says. "I decided to just stop it. I put everything I read right out there, on the table. Small triumph, but I had to do it or get swept up into this behavior I didn't quite get. I've now earned a reputation as the one who will read anything and everything no matter how graphic or gory or trashy or literary or unfit for human consumption. Murder, wife-swapping, whatever, they expect me to buy it. I'm free now. No one thinks, well, 'She's going to murder us' just because I read *The Murdering Wife.*"

"Even if the book is *nonfiction?*" Sherry asks, deadpan. Everyone laughs.

THAT THESE WOMEN hold within them the image of a wife who would not read or be seen reading certain books, and, further, that these books somehow threaten that image, shows us in action how the Witness's presence subverts women's own most innocent impulses. The thought "Be careful" overrules the natural urge to reveal her actions and share her feelings ("Hey, I'm reading this book"). She comes to suspect that her actions and feelings are somehow "wrong" or "bad," or at least threatening, and she covers them up.

By now we know who guards the image of that good and careful wife, but what does a book a woman is reading have to do with it? Why should what she reads have to be hidden from, or explained to, a loved one? Is it certain subject matter, or the very act of reading itself, that she feels compelled to "be careful" about? Is this, too, a holdover from the conduct books, which urged women to protect themselves from the stimulation of ideas?

Magda doesn't know the answers, but she knows she's "tired

of it. I don't want to have to explain anymore, 'Oh, it's just this new study, honey, nothing to do with *me*.' "

"Right," says Phyllis, forty: "If Bob notices the books I'm reading, *if,* I hate the way I actually rush in with an explanation, like, 'Really, honey, it's just a novel, I'm not going to go out and do what the heroine in this book does!' "

"I do it too," marvels Sherry. "It's reflexive: 'Don't worry, darling, it's about this woman who killed her husband's mother, but I promise I won't kill yours.' "

"No, no, he wouldn't blink if you read *that,*" Magda says softly, earnestly. "We're talking here, really, about sex books, aren't we?"

There is a barely perceptible pause. I want them to continue, but they don't.

"I hide *clothes,*" Sherry says brightly. "I hate having to account for a new dress, to say how much it is, to announce it or be grateful for it or *anything* for it. So I get weird. I just don't report it."

We're in more comfortable territory now. The group perks up.

"God, do I know *that* one," says Phyllis. "How many times have I had to listen to myself chirp, 'Honey, I just got the most *amazing bargain!* These little rags originally cost a billion dollars retail and I picked them up at this bargain basement, marked down twenty-seven times, and paid nothing at all'?"

Sandra interrupts to tell us about her trip, the day before, to Loehmann's, in the Bronx. "Just forty minutes away from where we are right now," she says wistfully, conspiratorially.

She is in the Back Room, she says, that section of the store that features markdowns of the most expensive clothes, the designer labels. Before she and Ted married eight months ago, she came here almost weekly to check out new arrivals, having been told that the Calvin Kleins and Donna Karans came in on Tuesdays, the Ralph Laurens and sometimes a Moschino or two on Wednesdays. Being a regular felt like being in a secret society: She could decipher the intricacies of the markdown process and knew precisely when to pounce or whether to wait. She knew the women who worked there; one of them called her when something wonderful came in or when it was marked down. Once she snatched up a Geoffrey Beene cocktail dress for $49.95, the coup of a lifetime. Thanks to Loehmann's, her wardrobe blossomed into just what it should be for her position as advertising director of a national women's magazine: classic, on the dressy side, but with the slightest downtown edge, just to prove she knew what was what. Her clothes reflected her persistence as well as her hefty salary.

Now, though, Sandra tells us, she agonizes over whether a pale blue cashmere twinset is too fashiony, but she loves it, and she buys it. On the way home, she finds herself anticipating what she'll say to Ted: "This designer I know had this amazing once-a-century sale, and I got this amazing deal . . ." But then she says to herself, Screw it: What am I doing this for? Why do I have to act as if it is my job to singlehandedly protect my husband from knowledge of the price of clothes? Why do I have to hear myself feign outrage not only at the price of clothes but at the terrible women who would *buy* them, when one of those terrible women is me?

The last time she bought something, she heard herself announce to Ted in a squeaky little voice that seemed to come up out of her from nowhere, "I got this at a fabulous sale! It only cost about a third of what it costs retail!"

She is angry now, not at Ted but at herself, at her compliance with . . . what? "Why, when I read in the paper or a catalog that a jacket costs a thousand dollars do I begin to make odd *wife* noises, like 'My goodness me! Just *look* at these prices! What a disgrace!'? And 'What kind of bad, profligate, spendthrift woman who has no respect for her husband's pocketbook or society at large would actually go to a store and *pay good money* for something that frivolous? Lordy, lordy me!' "

At home she takes the two little blue sweaters, still in the gray paper bag with the receipt stapled on top, and hides them under the bed. She has never done this before. She cannot bring herself to confess this purchase: She assumes that, even though it is her own money she is spending, money she has earned, Ted would just automatically be on the side of her guilt, confirming something about her that she is ashamed to reveal. They're both thirty-nine years old and working hard to support their home and their two-week yearly getaway, plus his two kids from an earlier marriage who are not yet fully on their own. The cashmere twinset feels to her, at this moment, like pure and utter *selfishness*.

That night, seeing her in her new sweaters, Ted says, "You look great! It's the first time I've seen you in anything but black! Is that new?"

"Old," she lies.

"So color is in again, eh?" he asks, distracted but attempting an interest in fashion for her sake.

"Pastels. Just pastels are in," she says gratefully, hugging him and wondering what it was she just put herself through.

HER RELIEF AND exhaustion have nothing to do with her husband, and Sandra knows it. The whole anxiety-filled trip she went on was not about her relationship with him. It was about her internalization of a specific standard of conduct, her attempt to mimic the ideal image of another wife than she who is—now watch her language—"more frugal, more industrious and serious, and less frivolous and idle and vain and selfish." It is not an uncommon feeling, this mix of obfuscation and guilty relief, this reflexive hiding and pretending. It need not be an expensive purchase that elicits it.

IN HER STUDY of the romance novel and the women who read them, author Janice Radway researched white, middle-class women from a suburban town she called, for privacy's sake, Smithton. The Smithton women, Radway noticed, often felt profoundly uncomfortable "over the amount of money spent" on these titles that brought them so much pleasure. Unlike Sandra, these wives were in fact "often called to task by their husbands for their repetitive consumption" of romances. The Smithton women felt their husbands' reactions were unfair. Their most common response was to defend themselves by pointing out that

> neither their husbands nor their children worry about duplicating tools, gadgets, toys or clothes they already have when they express interest in acquiring new ones. The women wonder, then, why they should have to adhere to standards of thrift and parsimony with respect to books when other family members do not observe the same requirements. Despite this sense of fair play, however, many of the readers still seem ill at ease spending money that they did not earn on a pleasure that is at

least questionable, if not downright objectionable, to their husbands.

Why would their personal choice of books be "objectionable to their husbands"—or their husbands' business at all? And why are the women "more comfortable with a picture of themselves as generous and giving mothers who would sooner spend money on other members of the family than on themselves"? Why, above all, do they seem "genuinely *troubled* by their simultaneous attempt to buy generously for their families and to admit their own need and right to spend on themselves" (emphasis mine)? According to Radway, "Every customer with whom I talked expressed some concern about whether she spent too much money on herself, and several even questioned me rhetorically about whether I agreed that they had a 'right' to buy things that gave them pleasure."

The list of anxieties harbored by these buyers of books about love and passion become evident as the women expressed to Radway why they are not free to please themselves, as other family members are. Their doubts about their own entitlement to pleasure—separate, private pleasure, unrelated to family—and their right to spend money on themselves suggests that the content or implications of these romances threaten not only their husbands (Why does she need to fantasize about love and sex? Isn't she satisfied in this marriage?) but also, more simply, the urge to have something pleasurable just for themselves. Their right to spend time and money enjoying an independent, not domestic, pastime is being called into question. The temporary withdrawal of attention from where it "should" be—on the needs and pleasures of everyone else—seems to leave family members feeling as hurt and indignant, and the woman herself as guilty, as if she had left her family outright. She has committed what writer Annie Gottlieb calls "attentional abandonment."

A strictly personal pleasure of her own is perceived as competing with, taking away from, the pleasure she gets from and gives to her family.

Does this sound familiar?

Each of these notions has its roots in the long-ago construct of the Wife, in the belief that a good woman finds her true and sole pleasure in pleasing others, according to the dictates of "natural" female character. Significantly, in the early nineteenth century women were also censured for reading for pleasure. Novels were regarded as "dangerous" because women might "get ideas" that would divert them from their duties, which would stimulate their presumably already overstimulated romantic inclinations.

"SO WHAT ARE we doing," I ask, "when we hide books or clothes or boast about our great sale purchases?"

We all look awkwardly at one another.

"My husband wouldn't be caught dead at a sale," says Mimi, rolling her eyes, and we all laugh. She sits up straight to affect a military stance and, walking across the room like a drill sergeant, mimics the motions of her husband in a men's clothing store, his unwavering purposefulness and clarity in buying, "bam, bam," just what he wants, with neither hesitation nor indecision. "He likes to walk in, have people wait on him, buy, get it all altered, pay the bill, leave, and have it delivered nicely steamed and pressed. It's retail all the way. It's a job. Like getting your driver's license. Barney's warehouse sale? Forget it. Too chaotic. He wants service. He wants fit. He barely looks at what it all costs. And he wants dignity and control."

Relief settles over the room again as Mimi acts out, in contrast to the parody of her husband's efficiency, her own "tortured, frantic, ambivalent, guilty, discount-store" clothes-buying ordeal, so lacking in dignity and control, so filled with desire and guilt.

The group lurches into the subject of men's behavior: how straightforward and unself-conscious it is, how uninvolved in these particular issues of selfishness versus selflessness, thrift versus extravagance, goodness versus badness, pleasure versus renunciation, giving versus taking, and we focus on the most delicious quality of them all: men versus women. If we can talk about what *we* do versus what *they* do, how funny and crazy *we* are, how weirdly forthright and unburdened *they* are by all the inhibitions and obligations that weigh on us; if we can laugh about this and not look too closely at ourselves, we'll be safe. As we lapse into that comfortable routine of us versus them, our relief is palpable, as soothing as Lucy versus Desi, Blondie versus Dagwood, and it no longer seems so strange that "they" must be protected from knowledge of how "we" really are.

In fact, whenever we become a little too conscious of our self-editing and self-censorship—the stashing under the bed of prices and pleasures, the terrifying anticipation of censure, the divvying up of purchases on different credit cards, all the apparatus of the complicated protection racket we're in—we collapse into an old, familiar girlishness to defuse it. As our stories of pleasure-sneaking get more rowdy and riotous—the clothes we hide more expensive, the boxes bigger, the sexy books more graphic or schmaltzy—we grow ever more comfortable with each other. *She does it too! She gets it!* We are sisters in an ancient, all-female club; we bond ever tighter.

We love to laugh about it, this "thing" we do. Here, with one another, where we make delightfully "outrageous" the very thing we do to divide, deny, and furtively gratify ourselves, the collusion feels like fun. We do not want to look at it too closely, so closely that it gets spooky. Subverting our desires into a shape we imagine to be more pleasing is funny and silly, a game, a harmless, feminine sleight of hand.

Investigating the subversion itself, on the other hand, makes us deeply uncomfortable. We do not like to consider it harmful, to us or anyone else. Better it be in the category of a white lie—adorable, ridiculous, essentially loving and lovable. We'd rather share daffy hiding and self-censorship stories than look at just what we're hiding and censoring, and why, whom we are protecting and for what reasons. And yet here it is, in one sentence: "I wouldn't want my husband to get nervous that I might leave," Mimi says.

Only through our laughter, it seems, can we normalize what's truly bizarre. It reassures us that what we are doing is pretending, not lying, and nobody will get hurt by our pretense.

We are nobly protecting ourselves and our husbands from pain.

"WHETHER THE INTENTION is to dazzle or distract, confuse or camouflage, masquerade or malinger, impress or impersonate, pretending is an ever-present adaptational strategy throughout all of nature," psychologist Harriet G. Lerner says, "allowing us to regulate relationships through highly complex choices about how we present ourselves to others." Because we distinguish between an act that benefits only ourselves and one that benefits others, we regularly make a distinction between lying and pretending. As Lerner says in her book *The Dance of Deception:*

When, for example, I ask friends to provide me with specific examples of lies they have told recently, there is an initial palpable silence. Not so when I ask the same friends for examples of pretending: "I pretended to be out when my friend called"; "I acted like I was interested in the conversation"; "I pretended that nothing was wrong when I had lunch with my folks." . . .

Not one person asked me to define my terms. People assumed that they knew when they were pretending, and to what end. Unlike other forms of deception, acts of pretending were described without defensiveness or apology, and with conscious recognition of their adaptive value.

Lerner notes the distinguishing feature of pretense:

First, pretending conveys the possibility—and sometimes even the wish—to fool not only others but also oneself. . . . Second, this word describes feigning or faking, but not stating a lie. . . . The third and most salient feature of pretending builds on the first two. Like sexual pretending, pretending in general (at least from the pretender's perspective) implies a *mild* act of feigning or faking that neither rattles the conscience nor demands careful examination. We don't typically associate the word with a shattering personal betrayal, a flagrant lie, or an unforgivable breach of trust. Rather, it calls to mind the suggestion that this particular form of insincerity or false appearance is personally okay or culturally sanctioned.

If pretending, or fooling oneself as well as others, is culturally sanctioned, and I agree with Lerner that it is, then the pretense these women and I are talking about is part of an entire ethos of culturally encouraged falseness. "The very word 'pretending,' like the word 'privacy,' " Lerner observes, "invites us *not* to pay attention to this behavior."

And in this shift away from looking closely at ourselves, just as in the shift away from being ourselves in front of our husbands, it *appears* that our dissembling is caused by men, is in some way all about them. But is it? We rarely question whether the men in our lives want our sacrifice. *Do they?*

These women say no, they don't. And yet they invoke their husbands as the explanation for their supreme caution, their vigilant conduct. When we hide the price of clothes from our husbands—"Men haven't a *clue* what it costs to *maintain*," Arlie dishes—is this a red herring, a diversionary issue hiding the fact that something far more vital about us is being hidden? And for reasons we don't understand?

Writer Mary Kay Blakely was in a talk-show audience when a woman spoke up about "her frustrations with domesticity."

Recalls Blakely, "She said, 'I would never tell this to my husband, but . . .' and 750 people listened to what this woman would happily tell strangers but wouldn't tell the man she loved." We believe this is normal; we accept the notion that a woman might really sooner reveal her marital distress to a television audience than to her husband. We assume that confiding certain truths in hundreds of female strangers really is easier than confiding in the man one lives with, sleeps in the same bed with, wakes up with every morning. What is the covenant? What's at stake here?

Ellen says, "This is where we all begin to say, 'Gee whiz, men are all babies, aren't they? Wow, what we gals put up with!' It makes it all so simple."

Phyllis faces Ellen. "Okay, let's take this seriously, then. What are you really doing when you hide a book? I mean, what if your husband were to say to you, 'Hey, what you're reading is disgusting; that book is completely revolting and I cannot believe any wife of mine would bring that trash into the house.' Is that what you fear? Is that the voice we're all hearing when we don't bring a book home?"

"Or else it's 'Don't you have something better to do with your time? Your money? Your mind?' " Ellen says.

Phyllis: "And do any of us have husbands who would actually say that, or even feel that?"

"No," Ellen says thoughtfully. "I'll get a question, maybe. A funny look. A crack."

"So if this is not a real voice, whose voice is it?" I ask. "Why do we hear it so clearly, and respond to it in this cowering way, superimposing it on our husbands' *real* voices? Why aren't we alert to it? Why don't we talk back to it? Why does it control us so?"

"I guess I'd say because it's easier to do what it asks, but that's a cop-out," Ellen says. "It's probably *not* easier, ultimately."

"Obviously not," I say. "Or we wouldn't be here."

Sherry adds, "Yes, and even if your husband *were* outraged, why not respond differently, with less guilt? We could answer by saying, 'I'm reading it because I want to,' or 'You read what you want, I'll read what I want,' or, if you really feel compelled to make nice, 'It's very interesting, honey; maybe you'll want to read it when I'm through.' "

"Why do we even have to come up with a legitimate retort?"

Diane says irritably. "We're being questioned about our right to read certain things, to have them at all, not just our right to display them. Something is putting our very entitlement on the line. I mean, we could strategize here forever about defensive blocks to incriminating questions, but why the hell are we being questioned?"

"And by whom?" I say. "Who is speaking?"

The group is agitated.

Sherry says, "Look, my husband is my friend; I discuss everything with him. So given that you've got a nonjudgmental ally, wouldn't you want to share what you were reading, or, at least, not be afraid to share it? Wouldn't you say, 'Look what I bought!' without expecting anger or censure or criticism or accusations about your selfishness or your extravagance? And, if he didn't want to read the book himself, I mean, couldn't we just say in our own defense, 'Oh, well, you don't have to enjoy it, but I will'?"

"Defense?" I say.

"That's just what I'm trying to avoid," Diane reminds her patiently. "I resent having to go through *any* of that. I don't want to have to justify myself."

"Well, hiding the book prevents you from having to justify yourself all right," Magda says. "But what's weird is having to justify yourself in the first place."

"We're being asked something much deeper than what books we read or clothes we buy." It's Alexandra, the psychiatrist, speaking for the first time, in a voice barely above a whisper. "It's not like anyone really has the desire or the power in 1997 to tell us not to read something. What we're being asked here is about something else entirely: It's about our intentions. The real ques-

tion is an intensely anxious one: Are you in this relationship totally? Do you mean to harm it? Swear you'll neither leave it nor
hurt it, never leave your husband nor hurt him nor betray him?
Are you totally and utterly faithful? And we're hypersensitive to that
anxiety."

There is another pause, a long one this time.

"We're protecting ourselves, I suppose," Ellen says wearily.

"We're protecting *them* is what we're doing," Sherry says. "Protecting them from what we're reading or thinking or doing or
planning or buying, lest something about our thoughts or our
plans or our actions make them unhappy."

"Make them unhappy and *what?*" I press.

"And make them mad?" Magda asks tentatively. "And make
them not love us anymore," she corrects herself. "And then we'll
be left all alone."

"And then?" I pour out the last drops of iced tea, now clear as
spring water.

"And then," Magda says, "we'll have lost everything."

Magda has come to the point. Remembering that women experience any threat to our most crucial bonds as not just a loss
of love, sex, and companionship but, as Jean Baker Miller puts
it, "something closer to a total loss of self," the preventive
actions—hiding, dissembling, pretending, lying—that seem so
senseless when we do them make profound psychological sense.
As women, our sense of self is integrally bound up in our relationships; we feel a moral imperative to make and maintain
them; this is *our job,* and our self-esteem is linked even today to
how well we do it. Our fears, all available studies suggest, revolve
around one and only one theme, the threat of loss. And if not
since time immemorial, at least since the eighteenth century,

women's behavior has been controlled with a code of wifely virtue and modesty to diminish this threat. Editing our self-presentation to conform to that code, justifying ourselves, however reflexively and unnecessarily, "protecting" men from knowledge of even the most trifling behaviors—it is all part of our defensive strategy, what we feel we must do to ensure that we are not left alone, that we do not lose everything.

And yet what I sense we're hiding most deeply, from ourselves as well as from the men we love, is the feeling that we have *already* been left alone. *What we fear most has already happened.* That's the paradox of women's conventional relationships and the work of the Witness. When Clara ceased to talk to Charles about her desire to go back to school, she abandoned her real, vital self, cut off contact, and wound up as isolated as a lost child. With cultural approval we've done it to ourselves, unwittingly exiled ourselves to an inner solitary confinement, in obedience to the Witness's perverse instructions and perhaps its support by our husbands. Because we are not aware of this, we feel it not as life-giving grief and anger, but as panic over the prospect of further loss. The reverberations of marriage shock are insistent reminders of the losses we keep feeling and then forgetting, experiencing and then covering, a layering of loss and denial that long preceded the compensatory "pretending" about our desires and pleasures that now seems so harmless and unimportant.

These wives are less anxious about a connection that might soon end (after all, not one of them really feels her marriage to be remotely in jeopardy) than they are, without knowing it, mourning a capacity for pleasure that already has been curtailed, an authenticity and expressiveness—in a word, sexuality—that have already been diminished.

An attempt to recover this lost pleasure accounts for the contraband books, the prohibited purchases, the women-only hijinks. I am convinced that if we don't recognize and feel, let alone mourn, those original losses, we will continue to view our clandestine consolations as benign behavior, something we women just *do*—a "girl thing"—that's ultimately inconsequential.

But of course, the consequences are many. Harriet Lerner says that, as she listens to women reveal how they pretend in their own personal lives,

> I hear stories of grave, ongoing deceptions. Of necessity, these must be shored up by lying and self-betrayal: "I pretended that I was in love with him, because I was desperate to get married"; "I pretended to want sex"; "I pretended to enjoy my motherhood"; "I pretended to be happy in my marriage." Patriarchy schools women to pretend as a virtual way of life, and then trivializes its eroding effects on ourselves *and our partners* [emphasis mine].

Finding it all too elusive to grasp, too embedded in our expert performance of marriage, we are now masters of the machinations ("So I just told him I was coming here tonight to discuss Proust"; "I charged the coat the way every salesperson in town recommends: to three different credit cards and handed her a bunch of cash") but puppets of the compulsion, unaware of the compulsion's source, its meaning, or its function.

Beyond the Witness's ready accusations of extravagance and

selfishness, though, lurks another, more insidious charge against us, not just about any pleasure but, specifically, about our sexual pleasure, for it is this above all about which the Witness is obsessed. "It is books about *sex* that we hide," Magda observed earlier, before we all deftly changed the subject, and she is right. Frugality, selflessness, industriousness: They're all up there in the pantheon of wifely virtues. But it is fidelity, chastity, about which the Witness rhapsodizes and hectors most on behalf of the institution of marriage and the men who designed it. The quintessential "goodness" of the Wife, after all, is her *sexual* goodness. Historically, her value—in fact, her *market value*—rested on it.

The real message of the Witness, the very heart of its righteous harangue, the whole point of its speeches about the joy of pleasing over pleasure, of selflessness over selfishness, of *moral conduct* as a wife's primary duty, is the crucial importance of our purity.

"I come back to the question of women's honor." It is poet Adrienne Rich. *"Truthfulness has not been considered important for women, as long as we have remained physically faithful to a man, or chaste."*

"She was intensely sympathetic." Virginia Woolf speaks scathingly about the Victorian Wife, immortalized as the "Angel in the House" in a poem by nineteenth-century poet Coventry Patmore. Woolf goes on:

> She was immensely charming. She was utterly unselfish. She excelled in the difficult arts of family life. She sacrificed herself daily. If there was a chicken, she took the leg. If there was a draught she sat in it—in short she was so constituted that she never had a mind or a wish of her own, but preferred to sym-

pathize always with the minds and wishes of others. *Above all,
she was pure* [emphasis mine].

It is lies and pretense about our *erotic* selves that go so deep we
no longer notice. Pretense about our pleasure—its intensity, its
rhythms, its idiosyncratic sources—is woven into our daily actions and expectations as wives like the threads in a patchwork
quilt. We lie to ourselves about it as well as to our husbands.

If we understood how dangerous it is to our psyches and our
relationships to edit our words, our thoughts, our actions, would
we begin telling the truth, piece by piece, thereby, in the words
of Rich, "opening the question of other ways of handling our
fear"?

If we saw that the real danger in "sheltering" our husbands is
the death of pleasure in our relationships with them, would we
continue to respond to an ancient voice droning on about false
dangers, threatening that we'll lose it all if we dare to be real?

Adrienne Rich writes:

An honorable human relationship—that is, one in which
two people have the right to use the word *love*—is a process,
delicate, violent, often terrifying to both persons involved, a
process of refining the truths they can tell each other. It is important to do this because it breaks down human self-delusion
and isolation.

It is important to do this because in so doing we do justice
to our own complexity.

It is important to do this because we can count on so few
people to go that hard way with us.

We can't count on our husbands to go that hard way with us, and they can't count on us to go that hard way with them, if we don't understand the nature of the protection racket we are in; the reasons why we decide, if we do, to conceal the contours of our pleasure. The truth about us will continue to be methodically siphoned off in the subtlest, sweetest, smallest ways—by us and unknown to us—unless we remember the terms of that ancient deal the Witness brings along with the Wife to the altar: Be as good and chaste and unthreatening as she and you'll be loved; be like you and you'll be left.

9

The Single Standard

Personally, I know nothing about sex because I've always been married.

—ZSA ZSA GABOR

WHAT IS IT about marriage that so often puts desire at risk?

The tension—some would say contradiction—between sexual joy and marriage is such a truism that a favorite question on book jackets and magazine covers is "Is there sex after marriage?" And inside the books and the magazines is advice on how to bring the spark back into your marital bed, counsel that often sounds labored, as if this will require *work,* like jump-starting a dying battery.

Is it familiarity that erodes desire, as so many believe, or plain old boredom? Is it rage or disappointment? Does desire get suspended in marriage somehow, put in a sort of limbo once that old psychoanalytic bugaboo, the incest taboo, is activated and the spouse becomes a surrogate parent, or sibling, or child?

I think there is another explanation, one built into the formulations of the institution of marriage. I wonder not "Where does the desire go?" but "Where is it located in the first place? Who has it? Who is supposed to be doing the desiring?"

Are we right in assuming that men's desire languishes when pent up in marriage? Or, the corollary, that the sexy woman they each married turned into the sexless Wife, one reason why we've historically excused men who have mistresses? Male desire, honored as something urgent, constant, uncontrollable, a biological force that cannot be contained, demanded that a parallel institution—adultery or prostitution—be built into the underside of marriage as a sort of escape valve, in order to protect it. Female desire, on the other hand—lamented, as recently as Shakespeare's time, as insatiable, an oceanic force far more inexhaustible than men's—left our vocabulary altogether during precisely that period when the Wife was being created.

For two centuries, women were supposed to be, by nature, above or without desire, able to enjoy sex at best only passively, "vaginally," and then only in marriage.

There has been great concern even in this century that women's enjoyment of sex could lead to total sexual chaos. "If she is normally developed mentally, and well-bred, her sexual desire is small," observed J. Krafft-Ebing at the turn of the century, in a book with the revealing title *Psychopathia Sexualis*. "If this were not so the whole world would become a brothel and marriage and family impossible." A similar concern consumed Dr. O. A. Wall, who wrote in his 1932 book *Sex and Sex Worship* that "a well-bred woman does not seek carnal gratification, and she is usually apathetic to sexual pleasures." Observing with relief that "lust is seldom an element in a woman's character, and she is the preserver of chastity and morality," he assured readers that if women *were* "as salacious as men, morality, chastity, and virtue would not exist and the world would be but one vast brothel." These beliefs would have astonished a Mughal aristocrat or a medieval cleric, or, for that matter, almost anyone who lived before the creation of the Wife.

Modern psychology has made a belated attempt to reinstall female desire, but somehow it doesn't quite *take;* there are always rules, instructions, diagrams, interpretations, as if making your heart beat faster were like programming your VCR. And there is that old problem of agency, that even the sexiest woman alive isn't really, well, aggressive with her desires; she wouldn't push a guy. The problem is one of point of view, as encoded in language. After three hundred years of the Wife's reign, the verb "to want" always implies a male subject. The Wife was constructed to be *without* desire, to have won, upon marriage, everything she could ever want, to be, within marriage, perfectly satisfied and sexually dead to the world outside it. The qualities ascribed to her when she (I always want to say "it") was constructed were the opposites, the absence and negation of those urgent, uncontrollable, unruly human qualities that are summed up in the word *desire.*

"I was walking down the street one day and saw a guy I went out with before I got married and I nearly fell over," a new wife laments. "He was *so sexy.* And I was *so married.*" Young wives tell me they're startled to experience sexual attraction for men other than their husbands once they're married, a reflection of their belief that marriage is not only the proper home for desire, but the only place it would even want to visit. "My old boyfriend still turns me on," a thirty-one-year-old woman is shocked to find, as if sexual exclusivity in marriage were innate rather than chosen, "which at first scared me. It made me question whether I really love my husband."

No wonder we have trouble imagining a wife desiring; the adored icon doesn't do it.

Try this experiment: When you think of the word *desire,* from whose perspective do you feel it? Your own—that is, a woman's? Just for a moment, try to conjure up images of a wife's desire— *her* pleasure, *her* desirousness. Imagine you are looking through this woman's desiring eyes at something sensuous and erotic. Close your eyes and picture what she sees, visualize what it is she desires. Do you see scenes or images of her sexual pleasure, or do you, rather, find yourself seeing *her*? Can you easily see from her vantage point, or do you keep looking *at* her from another one? Are you seeing, perhaps, a seminude woman, maybe elegantly presented, maybe just lying there, mouth shiny and open, eyes closed or glazed and blank, a picture of sultry invitation, zoned-out pliancy? Is this really a *desiring* woman, or is it one who is *desirable* to someone else? You wouldn't even *see* the desiring woman if she were the subject; you'd just feel what she felt, see what she saw.

Even for women audiences, the most potent image of "women's desire," is a woman ready for sex. Advertisers have used this picture to sell everything from laxatives to lipsticks. She's not *doing* anything, this woman we're to believe wants something; we can't tell what she wants, really—is it sex? Is it jeans?— or what she feels or thinks or sees, nor do we care; our interest in her is an outsider's interest, an outsider through whose eyes we have been trained to see.

And so *Women Who Love Sex* by Boston sex therapist Gina Ogden, a book, in the author's words, "about the right of women who have learned to say 'No' to abuse to say 'Yes' to pleasure," a book reflecting "my twenty years of feminist sex research," arrived on Ogden's desk before publication in a cover designed without her consultation. It was, she says, "something that looked like white-male-fantasy soft porn—a pinkly naked torso draped with a little lace." The book jacket was guaranteed, she felt, to "drive away the audience for whom the book was intended." Here was the same old automatic translation of women's desire into women's *desirability*, a conversion that in this case, Ogden feels, sabotaged the sales of her book.

She believes her audience, as well as her interview subjects, are women who love sex, act on their own desires, are the subjects, not the objects, of sexual fantasies—and did not require portraits of their own bellies and thighs in order to arouse either their erotic desires or their desire to buy the book.

If we ever really saw female sexuality through the eyes of women, we would see a far more erotically charged and richly textured landscape, a generous vista of pleasure that might even have beautiful *men* in it. There is a particularly female sexual bliss that writer Nancy Mairs has described as "a kind of potlatch in the world of orgasms," a uniquely female giving, expending, dispensing, and taking of pleasure without concern about ends or closure. The French feminists call it *jouissance*, a word that even *sounds* juicy; a word redolent of needing, savoring, wanting, lusting, craving, and receiving that has no English equivalent. If "women's sexuality" were really a term for women's subjective sexual desire, then whether that desire focused on men or women, it would look out from within a female body, through female eyes. Instead, like a spy, it turns around and gazes back at us, calling up graphic, clinical images of our genitalia, like those in pornography made by and for men.

You can see the art director's problem on that book jacket.

Let's see: Women who love sex. What to show? A man's body? No, women supposedly aren't turned on by pictures of male nudity. Hmmm. A man's face? Eyes closed, looking relaxed, hungry, aroused? No, that won't do either, everyone will think he wants his dinner. There seems to have to be a woman in the picture, as if a woman must see *herself* in order to believe there is desire. (I fought for years, when I was an editor at *McCall's,* to put a man on the cover, finally promising my boss that I would go to Hawaii and personally interview Tom Selleck, an old friend, but *only* if we put him on the cover. I did, and we did, and the sales were gratifying. Yet I had to win a battle against the historical prohibition of a man on a women's magazine cover, as if six million women would rather see themselves reflected back at them than a man.) More specifically, she must see her own soft and desirable belly, thigh, bosom, or buttocks, by now the only kind of image that encodes and signals sexual desire, even though it has nothing whatsoever to do with what heterosexual women might want.

No, the voice that says "I want" is not a woman's voice. The voice of her desire, that voice the late poet Audre Lorde called the "yes" within her, is not heard, unless it is her desire to fulfill the desires of a man. In marriage, we can imagine as a wife's desires only those focused on pleasing her husband and, later, her children. To visualize what she desires, presumably we merely need to see what *they* desire. Which is, of course, why we keep coming back to those images of *her.*

And so the world of women's desire is thought to be mystifying and unfathomable. Freud, of course, felt the sexual life of women, unlike men's, was veiled in obscurity, "a dark continent for psychology," at its heart the famously unsolved "riddle of femininity." What does a woman want? Did Freud frame that question back in 1933 because he really wanted to know the answer, or was it a rhetorical question to expose how ridiculously unfathomable and chaotic he felt the inner world of women was? By now, of course, the question itself, so hackneyed and overused, silences us. It's a joke. Most of the women I know, myself included, will evade it glibly: "What do I want? Hmmm. World peace. A new pink lipstick, not too shiny, not too matte."

For too long, asking "What does a woman want?" has felt like a trick question, at the heart of which is our understanding that to attempt to answer it sincerely is to be discredited; that wanting, real wanting, *itself* disqualifies us from the ranks of good wives. Married women have long understood that only one thoughtful answer to this infamous question is acceptable: to take men's desires upon themselves; to want what is wanted of them. All other answers sound threatening to a culture still hearing women's real voices as abnormally loud and "shrill," "strident," "demanding," "selfish," and "spoiled"!

We have accepted, or we pretend to accept, Freud's premise *that women wouldn't know what they really wanted if it hit them on the head,* so that it appears, as he put it, that "you are yourselves the problem"—and the riddle really *is* unsolvable. What does a woman want? Go ahead, I dare you. Give it a try. What is a wife's desire? Ummmmm, well . . . The real question is, who would venture to answer such a question? Who has the qualifications? Who would be believed? The implication is that the answers are as obscure as they were to Freud in 1933; or that the answers are (another male fantasy) terrifying; or perhaps, even that there really *are* no answers; that no matter how intrepid the navigator, you can't get to that dark continent from here.

Why else are girls' and women's erotic needs and feelings, their desire for pleasure in love, their joy in their sexuality, so emphatically an unwritten story? Surely we no longer consciously believe that women *have* no needs and feelings, that we *are* passionless by nature, or that we only want what others want of us. Surely we don't think the opposite: that we're utterly insatiable, a huge monstrous abyss. Is it, then, because we American women are sated, that we "have it all"—another popular answer—and so all our desires for love and family (and even foreplay!) are now fulfilled? That there's nothing to say?

But, then, why are women leaving marriages in droves? Is it that we are insatiable, and no matter how much we are given, we just want *more*? That, too, is a common belief. But if that's the case, what could be the "more" that we who "have it all" might crave so desperately?

These are the accepted explanations for the dearth of women's voices in the literature of desire and historically, I might add, in marriage studies. They're filled with experts, mostly men, interpreting women's behavior, speaking *about* women, but not to or with women. And so the explanations, of course, don't feel right. We *know* there's something wrong with them, yet there are no others.

What happens to efforts to speak our own truth, and our problems finding words to illuminate our experience, becomes clearer once we see what happens to what we do say. Remember how the word *erotic* in the title of my last book caused it to be banned in a retail-store chain? This surprising evidence of the banning of women's stories about pleasure, our erotic pleasure, encourages us not to bother to speak. It silences us. And in a cautionary tale right out of the most repressive Victorian con-

duct book, we find that when we do try to speak, even in a serious book, we will be censored.

You see the problem of looking at ourselves, at what we say or
read or buy, through others' eyes and words; how complex and
laborious it becomes to express our own desires and experience.
Once again a paradox lies at the heart of our silence: that
women are thought to be both insatiable *and* not desiring. The
world of women is at once a nunnery and a brothel.

WHEN THE KINSEY sex surveys reported over forty years ago that
50 percent of all husbands were unfaithful but only 26 percent
of wives, Kinsey himself, although attributing the discrepancy to
women's lesser sexual needs, noted that men were likely to overreport infidelity while women were likely to deny theirs, even in
confidential studies. In most studies today, the figures of men's
adultery are roughly the same as in Kinsey's time—approxi-
mately half of all married men—while the percentages of
women's reported adultery vary dramatically from study to
study. From under 20 percent in the 1994 *Sex in America: A De-
finitive Study,* 29 percent in the 1990 *Kinsey Institute New Report on
Sex,* to 50–62 percent in Dr. Bonnie Baker Weil's 1995 *Adultery:
The Forgivable Sin.* In these and other books, studies, and esti-
mates, the figure for men's adultery is higher. How could these
skewed statistics possibly make sense? With whom are all those
unfaithful men sleeping, if so few wives? Women outside the
country? Legions of tired, tawdry single women exhausted from
servicing most of the nation's unfaithful husbands as well as its
sexually active bachelors?

No: Men do and women don't volunteer their infidelity, even
to pollsters, today as in 1947, for the simple reason that men are

and women aren't forgiven for this sexual transgression. If men overreport still, it is because adultery remains a form of pleasure traditionally granted them, adding to their sexual appeal, enhancing the masculinity of the "cocksman," the "ladies' man," the Don Juan. And if women underreport it still, it's because this same act is taboo for a woman, undermining, not enhancing, her essential femininity and value, as the names for the adulteress—"tramp," "slut," and "whore"—make clear.

Too, men still stand to lose very little if they're caught in the act: A wife is encouraged to look the other way, to say "boys will be boys," to blame the other woman or even herself if her husband strays. But if a wife has an affair, she is to this day still in danger of losing her marriage, her home, her children, her financial well-being, and her social status; she will lose, this "bad" sexual woman, everything the culture offered her for being "good," just as the Witness incessantly forewarned. No one will be cajoled to look the other way if she has an affair; no one will be inclined to forgive her for her violation of this purity and her husband's trust.

We call it, this forked point of view that holds women to one kind of behavior and men to another, a double standard, just as we call a double standard that which prompts us to behave toward our husbands as if they were too fragile to be told what we read, spend, do, or desire. Look more closely, though, and you'll see that the "double standard" is really a single standard. Only one idea underlies our his-and-hers codes of conduct, and it is all about the distribution of desire: It's that men are more vulnerable to sexual need and betrayal than women are, and therefore it is women who must control and protect them. It is that one gender's nature and conduct is so imperious and at the same time so easily shattered that its survival requires the other gender to deform itself.

So complicit are we in protecting men's vulnerabilities, their honor, psyche, and sexuality, that to this day we sympathize more with their pain, even their imagined or anticipated pain, than with our own and that of other women, as we twist ourselves into knots to obscure and even reshape our desires. We are in thrall to this supposed male fragility because of the received wisdom about the consequences of ignoring it; we are told that one wrong move made by a wife can break a man, destroy a marriage, ruin everything.

Carolyn Heilbrun, in *Reinventing Womanhood,* laments our hypersensitivity on men's behalf:

> Woman has convinced herself that man, in whom society and the family invest all power, is mysteriously fragile. He is fragile not before other men, who may fight with him in the street, tackle him on the playing field, contend with him in battle; he is frail before women, and offers as the price of woman's selfhood his own intact sexuality.

Reminding us how incongruous is our simultaneous adulation and condescension—the emotional balancing act we saw in the last chapter, of which so many of us are not aware—she asks,

> Who can do justice to this riddle: man's superiority must not be challenged. It is a fact. At the same time, that superiority is so frail that woman must contrive with man to sustain it.

Why does she contrive with man to sustain it? Because

> sexually, women fear male impotence, fear any blow to the male sexual ego. At the same time that the male is raping and foraging on the streets, his counterpart, in bed with the

woman or in dialogue with the woman, is seen in constant danger of intimidation. The penis may collapse, crushing the male ego and the marriage in its flaccidity.

Bolstered by the single standard suggesting that, as Heilbrun says, the protection of the male is the "key to success for both partners in a marriage, not only literally, but figuratively," we hold women and not men responsible for all sexual misconduct. And we still, even now, after countless trials-of-the-century in every corner of the world, listen sympathetically as murderers drone on about having loved too much or "too well."

The single standard says that only men get hurt, so only men are really victims. (And if you hurt them, they'll hurt you, and in some way you'll have it coming.) It is through this prism of men's fragility and vulnerability that we view every move women make, in and out of bed, and it prevents us from speaking honestly about sex, in a survey, to each other, or, most devastatingly, to our husbands. Through it men are infantilized and women neutered: We're zookeepers, guarding and protecting our exotic, endangered, wild animals, making sure that nothing we do or say, read or think, know or feel threatens their security, and that, above all, nothing reveals our guilty yearning to burst out of this arrangement in which our pleasure, our desire, our power to stay or to leave—our *conduct*—is always, always suspect.

The terror is that if a wife does what she wishes (and here's where the notion slides in that she doesn't have any desires, or wouldn't know them if she tripped over them), everything else—society, the family, children—will go to hell; that only a wife's self-sacrifice assures reliable family bonds; her desire promises chaos and abandonment. This is an untested fear; the fact is that *the denial of this desire really is causing the chaos and aban-donment,* right now, as women initiate two thirds to three quar-ters of all divorces. We've got it exactly backward: We listen to the Witness to stave off a disaster that listening to the Witness causes. The woman's desire is what would persuade her to stay. Perhaps another framework, pleasurable and comfortable and roomy enough for both sexes, one that allows *both* of them their full sexuality, expression and transgression, goodness and bad-ness, would be more lasting. Rather than forcing her back to the zoo, where men are incorrigible so *somebody* has to be good, why not create another framework, one that assumes the morality and sexuality of both husband and wife—so she'll want to stay?

Can you imagine a marriage based on a new standard of sex-ual conduct, one that proclaims us all equally vulnerable, equally sexual, equally human? Can you envision an institution in which a wife's desires are acknowledged as real, as separate from her family's, and then openly discussed and acted upon? Can you imagine a time when seeing to wives' pleasure, our own separate pleasure, is crucial to the future of marriage?

Come join the revolution. We're about to overthrow the Wife.

10

How to Murder a Wife

"Ha!" she cried bitterly. "It is the old, dead morality."

"No," he said. "It is the law of creation. One is committed. One must commit oneself to a conjunction with the other—for ever. But it is not selfless—it is a maintaining of the self in mystic balance and integrity— like a star balanced with another star."

—Ursula and Birkin in D. H. LAWRENCE's
Women in Love

"I AM RUNNING across a field, past the grape arbor, past the peach orchard, through the tall yellow grass that shimmers in the dry California heat near my grandparents' little white clapboard house," remembers the heroine of singer/songwriter Roseanne Cash's short story "We Are Born." ". . . My grandmother is inside the house behind me, baking Scripture cake, which uses only ingredients found in the Bible. The ingredients themselves are listed in her recipe only by citation to each relevant chapter and verse, so someone less knowledgeable and virtuous than my grandmother would have to get out her Bible and look them all up. My grandma, however, knows them all by heart."

Immersed in a world where a wife's virtue is competitive and holiness her only currency, the narrator, at age eleven, already starkly sees her fate: to be as good as the baker of that cake and, like her, to know every one of those ingredients by heart. And so she runs, as fast and as far away as she can go, to a place less sanctified but more hospitable and alive, toward the railroad tracks, where the smooth warm steel under her feet "lets me know I'm really here."

"I run as if I would never stop," she tells us, breaking out the terms she sees for women and men in this story of love she wants no part of, "I run because I can almost see myself as an adult, and the murky vision terrifies me. I run because in the world in which I live, men are regarded to be irredeemably selfish and cruel, and women are unfailingly virtuous. I run," she says finally, "because I know I can never truly take my place in that picture."

Where can that young girl hope to find herself when she stops running? In what other picture can she truly take her rightful place? Can she avoid that still-life portrait of goodness and badness that is woman and man as she knows them, and the only model for love in the world in which she lives? And if she does, will anybody sympathize with her? Who will love her? How will she live?

The modern young heroine is asking an important question that we beg by telling her she'll understand when she grows up: Where do *I* fit in a world where sanctioned love, for women, means conventional goodness? *Where do I go if I want to love and be loved on my own terms?*

"There is no alternative to living within the structure," a thirty-year-old woman tells me matter-of-factly, acknowledging the same psychic double bind. "But how"—she shakes her head slowly back and forth—"can I live within such a structure?"

There you have it: the question I began my book with. And my answer is: You can't. To be among the estimated 35 percent of women who stay in a marriage longer than two to four years and survive—more, thrive—you will have to step outside the structure. You will have to enter love another way, through another story.

REMEMBERING JOHN GARDNER'S observation that every story begins with an arrival or a departure, the new story I want to tell begins with the departure of that Wife. "Successful plots often have gunpowder in them," scholar Jane Marcus has observed, and this one certainly does, because the heroine of that old tale will not exit gracefully. And if all else fails, she will have to be done away with.

Not that others haven't tried to do the deed. In 1942, when she was forty-nine and at the peak of her career, Virginia Woolf addressed a group of young professionals about the "phantom" who threatened to ruin her writing, that "utterly unselfish" Angel of the House whose cloying goodness menaced the integrity of Woolf's work. "I turned upon her and caught her by the throat. I did my best to kill her. My excuse, if I were to be had up in a court of law, would be that I acted in self-defense. Had I not killed her she would have killed me. She would have plucked the heart out of my writing."

Woolf threw innumerable ink pots at the Angel, but the creature's ghostly goodness kept returning, always managing to leave "the shadow of her wing or the radiance of her halo upon my page": She "was always creeping back when I thought I had despatched her." Woolf knew that for sheer staying power, the phantom's "fictitious nature was of great assistance to her." A flesh-and-blood creature can die, but a monster has the superhuman power to stay alive and well by lurking in the corners of the psyche.

It took Woolf years to kill her off, time much better spent "learning Greek grammar," she lamented, or "roaming the world in search of adventures." But she gave the task its necessary number of years, "for as I found . . . you cannot review even a novel . . . without expressing what you think to be the truth about human relations, morality, sex. And all these questions, according to the Angel in the House, cannot be dealt with freely and openly by women; they must charm, they must conciliate, they must—to put it bluntly—tell lies if they are to succeed."

As Woolf murdered the Angel so must we—each one of us, when we marry, kill the Wife, if she is not to kill our sexuality and silence our voices, our stories, our truths. Carolyn Heilbrun, too, once called for symbolically murdering motherhood, assuring appalled critics that "it is not *a woman* who is being symbolically murdered: it is the principle of motherhood. That principle, not its action in loving parenthood, but its establishment *as an institution,* must be demythologized and ritually destroyed" (emphasis mine).

Only the ritual death of the Wife will let marriage live. I am sure of this. The truly revolutionary act is not refusing to marry, but for those who desire marriage to insist on it without that false goddess, who still imperils our relationships as surely as she jeopardized Virginia Woolf's calling.

HOW DO WE begin? First, by admitting she exists. By understanding why she was created, and what and whom she serves. By understanding that her goodness only *looks* good, when in reality it is both unreal and deadly, like sugar-coated strychnine. And by understanding that her function was—and is—not simple: She is there to perpetuate a definition of the family that serves and nurtures everyone but the woman, and thus kills marriage at its core. Her smile suggests she cheerfully accepts this definition, thereby disguising, among other things, her inequality and loss of self.

By realizing that she lives on in us, casting "the shadow of her wing or the radiance of her halo" over our tentative, untold, newborn marriages. By identifying the voice of the Witness as it glorifies her, making sure her image and her static story with the storybook ending will loom larger and ring louder in our imaginations than any other possible tale.

Once we know that she lives, battening on our life, and understand how her goodness is reimagined and reproduced inside us, like a virus in a vulnerable host (hostess, I should say), we will be able to distinguish the Witness's voice from our own—and then from our husbands'. We can prevent the disconnections that cause marriage shock and that dissolve marriages.

By speaking the truth of our experience to our husbands and our friends, exposing what we are not supposed to see or know or say, we conspire with the men we love, behind the culture's back, to replot the tale. We turn our marriages into living works-in-progress, stories that shift and change and breathe as we do and have no prescribed endings. *Conspire,* after all, originally meant "to *breathe* together."

We need to bring our husbands into this experience of marriage shock so they, too, can watch what happens and how. Together we can see how the "morality" the Witness worships and the icon that represents it are a joint contrivance, a *thing,* an anachronistic piece of an outdated scheme. The evidence that we can no longer live in that scheme is clear from divorce statistics, but we will need to be revolutionaries to blast our way out of it.

THE HEROINE OF Margaret Drabble's *The Waterfall* is an author, Jane Gray, who has fallen in love with her cousin's husband, James, and is writing a novel to understand her passion for him. Jane is desperate to make sense of why her adulterous love "releases [her] from enclosure," liberates her from numbing alienation, and "delivers" her to a more complex, intense, and vital life and an authentic connection she has craved—when the "old novels" that instructed her since childhood taught her just the opposite: that sex condemns and silences women; that in fact "the price of love was death." The literary convention of the novel as she had always known it doomed her favorite passionate heroines to "drown in the first chapter."

Jane Gray blames this body of literature for its insidious hold on her vision of her own life. How inescapable its relentlessly punitive endings seem, and how powerless she feels to avert such an end! Novels have drummed into her such dread about her own future that she can't imagine any other finale than theirs: "Perhaps I'll go mad with guilt, like Sue Bridehead," she says, "or drown myself in an effort to reclaim lost renunciations, like Maggie Tulliver. Those fictitious heroines, how they haunt me." She is furious at the tyranny of a literary tradition whose heroines' gloomy fates cast a shadow of inevitability over her own life. "I worry about the sexual doom of womanhood," she says, "its sad inheritance."

What Jane attempts both as a novelist and as a woman is to set free a new narrative more welcoming to her own experience— what Anna Wulf in Doris Lessing's *The Golden Notebook* attempted when she, too, tried to break out of the old, punitive literary tradition for women who dare to transgress, "to over-step, to go beyond" the conventional story, to smash what Nathaniel Hawthorne in *The Scarlet Letter,* called "the iron frame-work of [men's] reasoning."

Searching for a way in which marriage need not be the end of women's story, and in which women's passion and voice do not mean their death, exile, or loneliness, Jane is overwhelmed. When, as Carolyn Heilbrun observes, "we live our lives through texts," how does a woman depart from those old stories by which she makes sense of her life? How does she reject the adored fairy-tale characters who lure her into the "happily-ever-after" ideal? And how will she avoid the tragic endings that befall women who try to break out of that story, endings she reads about daily in novels and newspapers, endings drummed into her by the Witness? How does she write her own life afresh, be-come the heroine of a new tale that opens on a more expansive reality than those two old alternatives offered women, conven-tional marriage or death?

Oddly enough, even our most radical and unconventional writers never imagined another story, nor offered another end-ing, as if unable, Heilbrun observes, "to see the failure of marriage . . . as something against which a woman might rise up," preferring "rather to defend the institution than examine it." Even a novelist as critical of social convention as George Eliot consigns her heroines to the most predictable endings, "condemning Maggie Tulliver in *The Mill on the Floss* to the stultifying society [Eliot] herself escaped," writes critic Gayle Greene. Poor Maggie renounces passion *and* marriage—both the bad-woman *and* the good-woman plot—but dies anyway, as if for simply failing to fit into any known plot for women.

Jane Gray scorns this finale but knows it will take everything she's got, both as a writer and as a woman, to escape it. "What can I make that will admit me and encompass me?" she wonders aloud. In a bold bid to rewrite the rules of the game, both in love and in fiction, she refuses finally to revise herself with "abnegation," "denial," "renunciation," those traditional feminine "virtues" inside marriage. Instead, she revises *them,* calling them not virtues but life-negating vices, evils that poison pleasure. Jane Gray does more than call "bad" what has for almost three centuries been worshipped as "good" in women: She constructs a radically new meaning of *good* to mean *good for her.* Reinventing language, questioning everything, she knows she must step outside the existing system to avoid the fate of the old heroines, to write a new life—knows, as Hawthorne did, that only outside the "iron framework" is there really life. "I will take it all to pieces," the driven Jane declares, speaking for all women who want marriage but want their own vital, pleasureful story, too. "I will resolve it to its parts, and then I will put it together . . . in a form that I can accept, . . . If I need a morality, I will create one."

If Jane Gray speaks for middle-class women, Roseanne Barr speaks for working-class women when she says precisely the same thing, twenty years later, about her own struggle: "While I'm alive on this earth, I'm going to create my own reality," she says. "I'm not gonna cut myself anymore to fit theirs. That's in all things I do, including my language."

Roseanne takes the sitcom form she inherited from Donna Reed and exchanges the smiling, selfless Wife for the hilarious "domestic goddess." Margaret Drabble does the same in *The Waterfall*, by smashing the form of the novel that was created just after the Wife was, the very novels that, Nancy Armstrong argues, "helped to redefine what men were supposed to desire in women and what women, in turn, were supposed to desire to be."

Jane Gray will abandon goodness and, like the women I met while writing this book, who love and lose and marry and struggle and transgress and remarry, will seek delight for herself as well as for her loved ones. The new heroines are out there, though the stories they are living have barely begun to take shape: Real women are insisting on their voices, their sexuality, fun, and adventure (*l'aventura* literally means "future")—insisting, in other words, on a heroine with a complex nature brimming over with anger and desire and power, and on their need and right to create a plot that thickens accordingly.

Taking the story of women's lives all to pieces and reframing it is not a job for the fainthearted. You must be clear. You must know the possible consequences. You must be as brave and radical as Jane Gray, an outlaw, a resister, daring to take your own unique marriage outside the "iron framework," into the open, into the world, out of the wintry landscape of the ideal.

Like Jane Gray, we are creating a new morality. To do so, we must discredit and then dismantle the old. We must ask: If the present morality, which centers on the Wife's goodness, is so good for us all, why are wives staging the most dramatic walkout strike the world has ever witnessed? Why, when women are working harder than ever both at home *and* in the workplace—sociologist Arlie Hochschild calls it a "double shift"—are wives still judged as harshly as in 1900, kept in line by the same accusations of "selfishness," the same questions about "femininity" and "morality," as our self-sacrificing foremothers were? What kind of morality is it if the conduct of men toward women, husbands toward wives, is not considered as important as the conduct of wives toward husbands and children? What are "family values," anyway, if one member of a family continues to be devalued yet paradoxically idealized? And how can one member be so deformed, not to mention depressed, without the others meeting the same fate soon after?

When our most respected theorists, psychologists, and sociologists have spent years pointing to the costs to women of their debilitating struggle against "selfishness," of carrying the full moral weight of the culture by shaping themselves into paragons of virtue, of taking responsibility for men's frailties and fragilities, can we now join them and say enough is enough? Why *not* risk the exciting possibility of authentic relationships?

We must totally rethink what we mean by the word *good* and consider, good for whom? What is a good marriage for *me*? What does a marriage of real mutuality look like, one in which my desires and pleasure are as paramount as his? If you were to try to imagine such a thing, what would a "wife's marriage" look like? Conduct books, old or new, don't care: Their concern is neither you nor your relationship, but your behavior.

What *is* moral is an institution that enhances the lives of everyone who enters into it and encourages the individual growth, distinctive pleasures, and unique desires of each partner as well as the joys they share. How can we call marriage "moral" when what is idealized in women and in men dehumanizes them?

In the past twenty-five years women have bloomed. How can we still be talking about fitting modern wives back into an ancient institution, rather than enlarging an ancient institution to make room for modern wives?

Will we assign virtue and power to both women and men? Will we factor into marriage the wife's pleasure, and see her delight and her quest for it not as "bad" ("selfish") but as good for her and therefore innately good—moral—not to mention good for her husband and children? And for marriage? As we enter the twenty-first century with the family in crisis, is this our one real hope for the future of marriage? I believe, as Marilyn French writes in *Beyond Power,* that "we act for our best selves when we strive for pleasure; we also give others the gift of those best selves as example, as encounter, and a source of pleasure to them."

THESE QUESTIONS INVOLVE more than a redistribution of goodness; they are questions about goodness itself. What is good? I'm going to call "good" in a relationship that which pleases and sustains the self, and to call "bad" those artificial qualities so long ago grafted onto the feminine ideal (and the masculine ideal, too, but that's a different book). We know from every study of women's psychology that not only do women find their characteristic, native pleasure in relationships, but that relationships thrive on pleasure. What I know is that wives' conventionally prescribed "goodness"—what we now call the "morality" that supposedly keeps entire families together—kills self, and then pleasure, and then, inexorably, relationship. The basis of a lasting marriage that delights the soul and that expands the self, women tell me, is pleasure. Pleasure comes from the old French *plaisir,* writes William Safire in his column on language in *The New York Times,* and "came into English and developed that sensual *zh* sound in the middle, similar to the pleasing *azure,* favorite of romantic poets. As a verb, it means 'to give sexual satisfaction to'; as a noun, it is not so lively as *delight* or *gladness,* not so rapturous as *joy, bliss* or *ecstasy,* and not so amusing as *delectation. Pleasure* is an emotion that suffuses one who has been gratified or stroked; it's a good feeling, whether physical or intellectual."

Any morality that does not include wives' pleasure is not "a morality," it is the single standard: It is a morality *tale.* And while there is some slight comfort in following its predictably cautionary program, just as there is comfort in pleasing others even when we don't feel like it because it's simply easier that way, or because we love them, or because our mothers and grandmothers did it, or because we get the Witness off our backs for a night or two, this is relief, not pleasure—a respite from accusations of selfishness, not joyful giving. The "morality" holding it together is based on what's presumed to be good for one of the partners and what's called "good" conduct in the other. Such an arrangement does not encourage such skills as conflict resolution, which experts find to be one hallmark of lasting marriages, and which assumes not only that conflict be acknowledged but expressed by both partners. Such a marriage is not one in which *either* partner can ultimately thrive.

It is, if one wants to be as forthright as Adrienne Rich advises us to be, a lie.

Unless we redefine goodness to mean what is good *for* wives, not what is good *in* wives; until we focus our attention on how wives are *feeling* rather than how they are *doing,* the very "morality" that has long kept marriages together will simultaneously strangle them. And women, I suspect, will leave them even more quickly and more often than they do now. Marriage will continue to exist—institutions rarely die—but will sink to the status of a sort of sanctified one-night stand, as modern women race into it for all the reasons women always have and then, shocked, race out. In response to this terrifying possibility, of course, the disapproving Witness will call for old "values" to be reinstated, the system tightened, and the rules regulating sexuality and divorce made stricter. Conventional wisdom will always assume that tougher laws and a return to "traditional values" are the key to those lasting marriages that elude us.

I clip newspaper items to this effect daily. According to a recent *New York Times* story, the Vatican issued a thirty-page document urging priests to better prepare couples for life together, contending that "permissive laws and the news media had created a climate that favors the breakdown of marriages." The document, the item continued, says modern society is marked by "an increasing deterioration of the sense of family and a corrosion of the values of marriage."

Tightening the controls, punishing slackers, blaming liberal lawmakers, the news media, or permissive sexual mores—any attempt to return to the system, to reinforce the iron framework—will only lead us back here again, precisely where the original controls brought us. No, the only way to save marriage is to revolutionize it, to make it serve real women. There is no going back. Our nostalgia about how "wonderful" marriage used to be is a wishful lie, like all nostalgia for "the good old days" when everyone stayed together forever, or when women were put on a pedestal, or when wives were adored, husbands respected, and God feared. There were no good old days for married women, as any glance through modern history will confirm. The glorification of marriage, the sentimental idealization of it, diverts our attention from women's real experience, shoring up the very system that women are quitting.

Marriage in America has always been in trouble; we have always been implored to save it. Amazed by the increased divorce rate, and alarmed at evidence that marriage was failing to such a great extent, William E. Carson wrote in 1915 in *The Marriage Revolt: A Study of Marriage and Divorce,* "What reforms will society bring about when, having recognized that certain traditional features of marriage no longer fit modern conditions, it seeks to adjust ancient conceptions to its growing need rather than its need to its inherited conceptions? What steps will it take to prevent unhappy marriages since it is unthinkable that society shall crudely content itself with treating the symptoms rather than the causes of the disease?" Fourteen years later, in 1929, the steps had not been taken: The alarmed authors of another marriage book, Ira S. Wile and Mary Day Winn, lamented in their *Marriage in the Modern Manner,* "The modern marriage, especially in America, needs saving, no honest observer will deny."

Since staying in a marriage has become increasingly optional, why don't we concern ourselves not with laws that make it harder to divorce but with relationships that will make the people who are unhappiest in it now—women—happier, so they will *want* to stay?

DOES IT UNSETTLE you to focus so intently on what's wrong with marriage rather than what's wrong with *you* for questioning it? Or does it relieve you? Is your impulse not to take seriously a discussion about the nature of marriage, the possibility of changing it? The injunction to not see, not know, not feel, and then not speak—the summary "goodness" of the conduct book's Wife—directs us to look for the problem within ourselves rather than in the system. If only we would try a little harder, the thinking goes, and love a little more, and go back to those old, comforting virtues, everything would be all right.

"If I'd only just go along with it, do what everyone says, perfect my body and my character, I wouldn't be so unhappy," you say. "I can *do* that. I'll just be quiet and not cause a fuss. It's smarter. It's easier. Who has time for this revolution? Who really cares? I'm not a revolutionary. I just want to get married, have a family, and get on with it. To make it work. I'm willing to just love him a little bit more."

No. You will not, cannot, have a genuinely good relationship that way. I know it sounds promising; it's supposed to. How can more love hurt anyone? I'll tell you: That's not love. You cannot pretend that the well of love within you is inexhaustible and so independent of the relationship you're in that it just erupts unconditionally, forever, needing neither reciprocation nor replenishing. That fantasy is one of the most seductive and insidious staples of a romantic myth that has long promised you bliss, safety, love, and approval, *if only you're good enough, giving enough, and selfless enough to earn it.* Pleasure fills that well. Pleasure, not self-improvement.

Love is not earned through endless giving; sainthood is. Marital love is mutual, connection, a relationship, not a one-way donorship. The latter is the very "morality" you're leaving.

"Love him more" is the battle cry of the Witness and of all those who idealize the Wife and make her the sole guardian of relationships. A facile formula for avoiding all conflict, it reinforces the spirit-killing lie that you should give more and want less, that your moral superiority should more than offset your losses. It is—and I cannot say this strongly enough—a sentimental and manipulative exhortation you must reject if you hope to end that endless cycle of "doing good and feeling bad" that psychologist Jean Baker Miller has observed in so many women.

Self-improvement is immensely seductive—God knows every inch of women has been scrutinized, criticized, and measured, altered in the name of winning more love—but it will only sabotage, not ensure, the loving marriage you want. Conventional wisdom will always insist otherwise, because its "wisdom" is broadcast to you from right inside the very structure you're challenging. Step outside that framework. Better yet, don't even go in. You can have marriage without following such pleasure-negating rules.

You are not a moral project, made ever better by more and more giving, less and less wanting. The betterment of *you*, morally (and physically, too), only reinforces the single standard that declares men uncontrollable and unalterable and you endlessly flexible, responsive, and accommodating. This is the very bargain that has left you in marriage shock, feeling all alone and wondering why you're trying so hard while the Witness, breathing down your neck, urges you to try harder still.

We know who needs marriage and who does not; who flourishes in marriage and who does not; who is currently threatened by its breakdown and who is not. Isn't it interesting that the culture still turns its eye accusingly, beseechingly toward woman to save the social order—by fixing and changing not it but *her*?

Until we fully and truly take this in, we will be vulnerable to the authority of the Witness and to the peculiar psychological games it exalts. We will continue forlornly hoping to collect on its three-centuries-long promissory note.

We must remember that the ideal Wife never existed but was a symbol of loss, the deprivation of the fuller relationship couples had before separate spheres divided them and the fuller lives women had when they took part in craft and commerce. We no longer need her, this icon, this monster: To emulate her manipulative, self-sacrificing, silent goodness is to split off from our humanness and our husbands, to split off from our deepest selves and joy, to be false to our relationships. Love split off from power and productivity is not love at all, but a wrenching separation of home from world, of women from men, of soul and body from mind. It leaves men and women stranded in different channels of giving and taking, groping for each other with the diminished resources allotted each of them in the split. It leaves us all thinking we speak different languages, come from different planets, and cannot possibly connect.

Let's replace that stern, rigid, either-or language we hear when we marry, the voice of the Witness, with the voice of our authentic selves, our more fluid sensibility. Let us bring into the dialogue of our marriages the distinctive "babel of eroticism, attachment, and empathy"—that powerful, flowing, oceanic delight that women take in their relationships and pour back into them, the language that Nancy Mairs says is ours uniquely. Inside the present framework, such a word as *jouissance* will never have an English translation. Such a female language, with its fluid, emotional tones and its extensive three-octave range—the capacity for fun and joy, the sheer unself-conscious expressiveness of it—cannot even be imagined. The full range of female pleasure is as unlikely to be celebrated inside the institution of marriage as Mardi Gras is in the military. A wife must rush out of doors, go AWOL, or she will be silenced.

FOR A GLANCE into who is and who isn't choosing marriage specifically for pleasure, *New Woman* senior editor Stephanie von Hirschberg and I surveyed the magazine's readers. In our October 1994 questionnaire, we asked if anyone out there thought the primary purpose of marriage is *to have fun*. Other choices included: to raise a family; to foster spiritual growth; to build character; to be financially stable.

The results: Of the five thousand women who responded, those who chose "having fun" as the primary purpose of marriage were most likely to call their marriages "great."

They enjoy the best sex, get the most respect and attention from their husbands, think the least about divorcing, and would marry the same men all over again. In short, by all measures available, they have the most fun!

Yet, despite the clear and direct connection between valuing fun in marriage and having it, and the deeper and more global marital contentment claimed by those who chose it, a distinct minority of readers—fewer than a third in every age group—actually marked the "fun" option.

In the light of this discovery, readers' inclination to trivialize fun becomes not baffling but sad, a powerful reminder of where pleasure fits into our hierarchy of values. Many of us still feel we betray our frivolity, our immaturity, to say outright, "What I want most is to have a fun, sexy thing going with my partner," yet the evidence is that it is the surest way to the deep commitment, profound trust, and close, spiritual bond we *also* want in marriage. Words like *honor* and *duty, forever* and *compromise;* phrases like "settling down" and "taking responsibility"—our good conduct—have a way of adding such weight to what started out as an easy, fluid, breathing relationship that by the time *family* and *children* and *values* get thrown in, we begin to believe that pleasure is "selfish." Which is too bad. Because it isn't. Fun is sexy. It's life-affirming. It's subversive. It's possibly what made you a couple in the first place. The reason so many women sense the Witness hovering when they choose pleasure, I suspect, is because that indescribable bond strengthens that couple so, puts them outside the culture's dictates, a bit more removed from notions of who they should be as married people and how they should behave.

What's more, it turns out that pleasure, rather than being something you can have for dessert once a month after loftier, worthier goals are met, seems instead to be the shortest route to these goals. Fun turns into trust; fun creates respect; fun produces a spiritual bond; fun generates intimacy. Seen this way, as a vital catalyst rather than an optional frill, fun—pleasure in relationships—is hardly trivial.

How do children learn, after all? Through hours of play. What is good sex? *Adult* play. In all these letters that point to pleasure as the prime ingredient in their marriages, not merely a spice, I see a view of marriage that one doesn't often get to see—the fun part.

"BUT TRADITIONAL MARRIAGE works wonderfully for some people," you will be told. Of course it does. Before you get misty-eyed, though, I guarantee that those people for whom the old framework appears to work wonderfully have hacked away at it, enlarged it from within. They had a crisis that forced them to reimagine their roles, rethink their relationship, reclaim their voices and their lost selves and renegotiate the contract. The particulars of the crisis are unimportant: when the babies went off to school, or the children left home, or husband or wife had an affair; depression or a job loss or the death of a friend. But in every lasting marriage I have ever observed, there was a crisis, and it was usually a woman who said, "I can't do it this way any longer," and negotiated different terms.

What I want for you, however, is that you go into marriage in such a way that *re*trieving and *re*claiming are not automatically necessary because the crisis that broke the system's grip was averted; the system never *got* a grip on you. This is not to say you'll never want to reevaluate or rethink your relationship years later, or renegotiate terms that no longer suit you down the line. But if you know about the perils of marriage shock, if you are aware of the way the Witness confronts you with an icon of perfection that can do nothing but harm to you and to your relationship, you will never revise yourself into a Wife in the first place. You will bring your whole self, your usual conduct, into marriage. Marriage shock can be a thing of the past only when we conspire with our husbands to see the dangers of the old framework, subvert it, get outside it, create another structure. Family therapist Thelma Jean Goodrich, passionate about the responsibility of therapy to fix marriage rather than just the married, says that therapists must position themselves differently. In her essay "Women, Power, and Family Therapy: What's Wrong With This Picture?" she writes:

> Any fundamental change in marriage requires that it be moved from the realm of power into the realm of pleasure where mutuality and reciprocity replace hierarchy and control. Such a shift is constrained, however, by the unequal power in the world for men and women. The constraint is there even when the shift is fervently desired by both partners—a desire which is itself constrained by unequal power in the world. It is important that we acknowledge this limitation so that we do not mystify ourselves and our clients.

A warning: As we, together with our husbands, coauthor new plots and create our own deeply personal, unconventional scripts and narratives, we will find it hard going. We will feel lost on our uncleared path, without familiar, comforting markers. And we will surely be called "selfish," "stupid," and "crazy."

Our decision not to find pleasure the old-fashioned way—by giving it up—is disruptive to an old-fashioned order of things, and we will be called names. The Witness doesn't tell us what will work best for us only what society calls "good." Yet, a woman from Idaho tells me she doesn't sleep in the same bed as her husband. A woman from Indiana says she doesn't even live in the same *state*. These arrangements happen to work for these women, to keep their marriages vital and alive. Their families and friends disapprove. This disapproval keeps the Witness in its pulpit, shouting its sermon. This disapproval sustains the nagging belief that the Wife exists, that she's out there, somewhere, in that mythical perfect marriage, doing everything perfectly, cheerfully following ten neat rules to a more perfect marriage. Can you give up the desire to be idealized? Can you tolerate disapproval? Being thought of as "not having a good marriage" or as "weird"? Or as "negative" for rejecting those unrelentingly upbeat but clearly useless prescriptions? Can you handle being thought, even, "a bad woman"?

In all my work I've found that what a woman wants—Freud's infamous riddle—is not the idealized roles and relationships the fairy tale promised her, but the ordinary, ongoing attachments in which she can be herself, taking her great pleasure in her relationships, both in and outside of her marriage. Women in the most satisfying relationships feel free to expand, want, explore, be themselves, pursue their own stories—and, not surprisingly, they are in the least conventional marriages. They have killed off the Wife and stifled the Witness and live in troublesome, triumphant, connected, struggling relationships. They do not idealize marriage, but place it on a continuum with their long and wide experience of other relationships. They have dared to take the framework all to pieces and to construct a morality for themselves, to write themselves fully into roomy, pleasurable, singular marriages.

If you have the courage to do this, I promise you a marriage that satisfies the soul—and therefore joy, but I also must warn you of one unexpected consequence: Reinventing the word *wife* in your own image is, like any creative act, hard and painful work. Virginia Woolf, in her diary, reminds us of the emotional cost of letting go, of being a pioneer. Do not, she advises, expect to go against the tide of conformity without sadness:

> If one is to deal with people on a large scale & say what one thinks, how can one avoid melancholy? I don't admit to being hopeless though—only the spectacle is a profoundly strange one; & as the current answers don't do, one has to grope for a new one; & the process of discarding the old, when one is by no means certain what to put in their place, is a sad one.

Joy and sadness, however, are not contradictory; they are both parts of authentic feeling—unlike the false smile on the Wife's face.

ACKNOWLEDGMENTS

MY SPECIAL THANKS to the women who spent so much time with me over a period of years, searching for words to reveal themselves and their experience. I feel sure their work and struggle will, as they hope, help other wives and husbands.

I am deeply grateful to Annie Gottlieb, on whom I depended not only to help me process, map, and formulate all that I learned, but much more: to bring such intense material to life when its substance and meaning often felt—as it did to the women themselves—too slippery to unearth and articulate. I'm especially grateful, too, to Elizabeth Debold: Her deep understanding of this work, and the ideas and knowledge and guidance she provided from the project's inception to its conclusion, have enriched the book immeasurably. My great thanks to my agent and friend Joni Evans, who counseled and supported me, as always. Ruth Fecych, my editor, encouraged me to write the book I wanted to write, never once revealing whether this prospect worried her or my publisher, and I thank her.

I'm indebted to Jack DeWitt for listening, agreeing, and rebutting, finding material for me, sharing his library. Lesley Dormen, Carol Gilligan, Eileen Ryan, Judith Stone, and Eileen Winnick read different versions of the manuscript and offered invaluable suggestions and improvements.

Special thanks to my mother, Ethel Heyn, who came to my rescue with emotional support throughout the project, and with research when I was on deadline.

Many others have reached out to help me in so many thoughtful and important ways, each crucial to this book and to me: Natalie Robins; Christopher, Rachel, and Noah Lehmann-Haupt; Laura Zigman; Jean Baker Miller; the late Jessie Bernard; Amy and Art Cooper; Beth Pearson; Richard Dawkins; Jacques Sandulescu; Jorge Stolkiner; Heather Willihnganz; Ken Dornstein; Kathryn Geismar; Jeryl Brunner; Emily Listfield; Betsy Israel; Carol Randel; Connie Titone; Sarah Rosen; Margaret Wimberger and Byron Dobell; Alex Mayes Birnbaum. Thank you.

The Writers Room, where I began this book, provided the peace and solitude I needed to launch much of this work. Thank you, Donna, Andrew, Bill, and Al.

SELECTED BIBLIOGRAPHY

Armstrong, Nancy. *Desire and Domestic Fiction: A Political History of the Novel.* New York: Oxford University Press, 1987.

————, and Tennenhouse, Leonard, eds. *The Ideology of Conduct: Essays in Literature and the History of Sexuality.* New York: Methuen & Co., 1987.

Austen, Jane. *Pride and Prejudice.* New York: Holt, Rinehart & Winston, 1949.

Barreca, Regina. *Perfect Husbands (& Other Fairy Tales): Demystifying Marriage, Men, and Romance.* New York: Harmony Books, 1993.

Belenky, Mary, et al. *Women's Ways of Knowing: The Development of Self, Voice and Mind.* New York: Basic Books, 1986.

Bernard, Jessie. *The Future of Marriage.* New York: World Publishing, 1972.

Betts, Edwin Morris, and Beam, James Adam, Jr., eds. *The Family Letters of Thomas Jefferson.* Columbia, Mo.: University of Missouri Press, 1966.

Bok, Sissela. *Lying: Moral Choice in Public and Private Life.* New York: Vintage Books, 1978.

Cancian, Francesca M. *Love in America: Gender and Self-development.* Cambridge, England: Cambridge University Press, 1987.

Cash, Roseanne. *Bodies of Water.* New York: Hyperion, 1996.

Cogan, Frances B. *All-American Girl: The Ideal of Real Womanhood in Mid-Nineteenth-Century America*. Athens, Ga.: University of Georgia Press, 1989.

Coontz, Stephanie. *The Way We Never Were: American Families and the Nostalgia Trap*. New York: Basic Books, 1992.

Cott, Nancy F. *The Bonds of Womanhood: "Woman's Sphere" in New England, 1780–1835*. New Haven: Yale University Press, 1977.

———, ed. *Root of Bitterness: Documents of the Social History of American Women*. New York: E. P. Dutton & Co., 1972.

———, and Pleck, Elizabeth H. *A Heritage of Her Own: Toward a New Social History of American Women*. New York: Simon & Schuster, 1979.

Dawkins, Richard. *The Selfish Gene*. New York: Oxford University Press, 1976.

Debold, Elizabeth; Wilson, Marie; and Malave, Idelisse. *Mother-Daughter Revolution: From Good Girls to Great Women*. New York: Addison-Wesley, 1993.

DeWitt, Paula Mergenhagen. "Breaking Up Is Hard to Do," *American Demographics: Marriage and Divorce*, 1994.

Douglas, Ann. *The Feminization of American Culture*. New York: Alfred A. Knopf, 1977.

Drabble, Margaret. *The Waterfall*. London: Weidenfeld and Nicolson, 1969.

Ehrenreich, Barbara. *The Hearts of Men: American Dreams and the Flight from Commitment*. New York: Anchor Books, 1983.

———, and English, Deirdre. *For Her Own Good: 150 Years of the Experts' Advice to Women*. New York: Anchor Books, 1978.

French, Marilyn. *Beyond Power: On Women, Men, and Morals*. New York: Summit Books, 1985.

Friedan, Betty. *The Fountain of Age*. New York: Simon & Schuster, 1993.

Gaitskill, Mary. *Bad Behavior*. New York: Vintage Books, 1989.

Gallagher, Maggie. *The Abolition of Marriage: How We Destroy Lasting Love*. Washington, D.C.: Regnery Publishing, 1996.

Gilligan, Carol. *In a Different Voice: Psychological Theory and Women's Development.* Cambridge, Mass.: Harvard University Press, 1982.

Greene, Gayle. "Margaret Drabble's *The Waterfall:* New System, New Morality" in *Novel,* Fall 1988.

Gleick, Elizabeth. "Should This Marriage Be Saved?," *Time,* February 27, 1995.

Goodrich, Thelma Jean, ed. *Women and Power: Perspectives for Family Therapy.* New York: W. W. Norton and Co., 1991.

Heidenrich, Sandra Leah. "Bridal Blues: Depression in Newlywed Women," master's thesis at Pacifica Graduate Institute, Santa Barbara, California, 1990.

Heilbrun, Carolyn G. *Writing a Woman's Life.* New York: Ballantine Books, 1989.

———. *Hamlet's Mother and Other Women.* New York: Columbia University Press, 1990.

———. *Reinventing Womanhood.* New York: Norton, 1981.

Hymowitz, Carol, and Weissman, Michaele. *The History of Women in America.* New York: Bantam Books, 1978.

Jack, Dana Crowley. *Silencing the Self: Depression and Women.* Cambridge, Mass.: Harvard University Press, 1991.

Jordan, Judith V., et al. *Woman's Growth in Connection: Writings from the Stone Center.* New York: Guilford Press, 1991.

Kaschak, Ellyn. *Engendered Lives: A New Psychology of Women's Experience.* New York: Basic Books, 1992.

Lahr, John. "Dealing with Roseanne," *The New Yorker,* July 17, 1995.

Lerner, Harriet G., Ph.D. *The Dance of Deception: Pretending and Truth-telling in Women's Lives.* New York: HarperCollins, 1993.

Levinson, Daniel J. *The Seasons of a Woman's Life.* New York: Alfred A. Knopf, 1996.

Mairs, Nancy. *Voice Lessons: On Becoming a (Woman) Writer.* Boston: Beacon Press, 1994.

Mauthner, Natasha. "Postnatal Depression: A Relational Perspective," doctoral thesis at Cambridge University, 1984.

McGrath, Ellen. *When Feeling Bad Is Good*. New York: Henry Holt, 1992.

Miller, Jean Baker. *Toward a New Psychology of Women*. Boston: Beacon Press, 1976.

Miller, Nancy K. *Subject to Change: Reading Feminist Writing*. New York: Columbia University Press, 1988.

Newton, Judith Lowder, "Power and the Ideology of 'Woman's Sphere' " from *Women, Power, and Subversion: Social Strategies in British Fiction 1778–1860*. In *Feminisms: An Anthology of Literary Theory and Criticism*, Robyn R. Warhol and Diane Price Herndl, eds. New Jersey: Rutgers University Press, 1991.

Nolen-Hoeksema, Susan. *Sex Differences in Depression*. Stanford, Cal.: Stanford University Press, 1990.

Norton, Mary Beth. *Liberty's Daughter: The Revolutionary Experience of American Women, 1750–1800*. New York: Little, Brown & Company, 1980.

Ogden, Gina. "Media Interruptus: Sexual Politics on the Book Tour Circuit," *Ms.*, November/December 1995.

———. *Women Who Love Sex*. New York: Pocket Books, 1994.

Postman, Andrew. "Professor of the Paranormal," *Mirabella*, July 1996.

Radway, Janice A. *Reading the Romance: Women, Patriarchy and Popular Literature*. Chapel Hill, N.C.: University of North Carolina Press, 1991.

Reich, Charles A. *Opposing the System*. New York: Crown, 1995.

Rich, Adrienne. *On Lies, Secrets and Silence, Selected Prose, 1966–1979.* New York: Norton, 1979.

Rothman, Sheila M. *A Woman's Proper Place: A History of Changing Ideals and Practices, 1870 to the Present*. New York: Basic Books, 1978.

Rothstein, Edward. "Technology" column in *The New York Times,* June 10, 1996.

Scarf, Maggie. *Unfinished Business: Pressure Points in the Lives of Women*. New York: Ballantine Books, 1980.

Schwartz, Pepper. *Peer Marriage: How Love Between Equals Really Works*. New York: The Free Press, 1994.

Segal, Lore. Review of Jamaica Kincaid's *The Autobiography of My Mother* in *The Nation,* February 5, 1996.

Sheldrake, Rupert. *The Presence of the Past: Morphic Resonance and the Habits of Nature.* New York: Times Books, 1988.

Skolnick, Arlene. *Embattled Paradise: The American Family in an Age of Uncertainty.* New York: Basic Books, 1991.

Smith-Rosenberg, Carroll. *Disorderly Conduct: Visions of Gender in Victorian America.* New York: Oxford University Press, 1985.

Stibbs, Anne. *A Woman's Place: Quotations about Women.* New York: Avon Books, 1993.

Tannen, Deborah, Ph.D. *You Just Don't Understand: Women and Men in Conversation.* New York: William Morrow & Company, Inc., 1994.

Ulrich, Laurel Thatcher. *Good Wives: Image and Reality in the Lives of Women in Northern New England, 1650–1750.* New York: Vintage Books, 1991.

Wallerstein, Judith. *The Good Marriage.* New York: Houghton Mifflin, 1995.

Welter, Barbara. *Dimity Convictions: The American Woman in the Nineteenth Century.* Athens, Ohio: Ohio University Press, 1976.

Woolf, Virginia. *The Diary of Virginia Woolf,* vol. 1, 1915–1919. Anne Olivier Bell, ed. New York: Harcourt Brace Jovanovich, 1977.

———. "Professions for Women," in *The Death of the Moth and Other Essays.* New York: Harcourt Brace Jovanovich, 1942.

———. *A Writer's Diary.* New York: Harcourt Brace Jovanovich, 1954.

A selection of conduct books and letters:
The Duties of Women: A Course of Lectures, by Frances Power Cobbe, 1898; *Maxims for Married Ladies,* letter XVIII, 1796; "A Letter to a Very Young Lady on Her Marriage," by Dean Swift, from *Advice to the Fair Sex; in a Series of Letters on Various Subjects,* by a Gentleman in This City, to his Niece in Cork, 1803; *A Father's Legacy to His Daughter,* by John Gregory, 1774; *Woman Suffrage Wrong,* by James McGrigor Allan, 1890; *The Whole Duty of Woman,* by William Kenrick, 1807; *Sesame and Lilies,* by John Ruskin, 1865; *A Plan for the Conduct of Female Education in Boarding*

Schools, by Erasmus Darwin, 1798; *An Enquiry into the Duties of the Female Sex,* by Thomas Gisborne, 1798; *Sketches of American Character,* by Sarah Josepha Hale, 1829; *Manners; or, Happy Homes and Good Society All the Year Round,* by Mrs. Hale, 1868; *The Women of England,* by Sarah Ellis, 1839; *Letters to a Daughter,* by Wm. B. Sprague, 1834; "My Mind and Its Thoughts," in *The Sexes,* by Sarah Wentworth Morton, 1823; *Sermons to Young Women,* by James Fordyce, 1794; *Manners for Men,* by Mrs. Humphry ("Madge" of "Truth"), 1897; *How to Be Happy Though Married,* by Rev. E. J. Hardy, 1886; *Manners Makyth Man,* by Rev. E. J. Hardy; *Advice to Young Men and (incidentally) to Young Women, in the Middle and Higher Ranks of Life,* by William Cobbett, 1831; *Advice to Young Men on Their Duties and Conduct in Life,* by T. S. Arthur, 1848; *Manual for Young Ladies,* by C. H. Kent, 1881; *The Lady's Pocket Library,* 1809.